No Comment

No Comment

What I Wish I'd Known About Becoming A Detective

JESS McDONALD

RAVEN BOOKS

LONDON · OXFORD · NEW YORK · NEW DELHI · SYDNEY

RAVEN BOOKS
Bloomsbury Publishing Plc
50 Bedford Square, London, WC1B 3DP, UK
29 Earlsfort Terrace, Dublin 2, Ireland

BLOOMSBURY, RAVEN BOOKS and the Raven Books logo are trademarks
of Bloomsbury Publishing Plc

First published in Great Britain 2023

Edited and revised by Victoria Millar

Names and details of individuals as well as places and locations in this book have been
changed to preserve their anonymity

A catalogue record for this book is available from the British Library

ISBN: HB: 978-1-5266-2170-2; eBook: 978-1-5266-2172-6;
ePDF: 978-1-5266-5232-4

2 4 6 8 10 9 7 5 3 1

Typeset by Newgen KnowledgeWorks Pvt. Ltd., Chennai, India
Printed and bound in Great Britain by CPI Group (UK) Ltd, Croydon CR0 4YY

To find out more about our authors and books visit www.bloomsbury.com
and sign up for our newsletters

Dedicated to my Mum (Mama), Dad (Pops) and family (old and new, the lot of you!) for your incredible support.

Contents

1

A Voluntary Shot to the Face

Summer 2018

Today is a big day at Police School. It's the last day of our Officer Safety Training (OST) – a five-day physical class involving applying handcuffs, handling weapons and learning self-defence. We're hoarse from yelling 'GET BACK' at each other and our instructors as we hone our new techniques. To celebrate completing OST, we're going to be sprayed in the face with CS tear gas.

CS gas, chlorobenzalmalononitrile, is a chemical weapon which is illegal and classed as a firearm in the UK. The police would only use it as a tool of last resort in the most extreme circumstances, in other words, when there is a threat to an officer's life. The chemical leaves those sprayed with it incapacitated by pain and temporarily unable to see. Now is our chance to experience first-hand exactly how that feels.

I am not at all sure about this.

I'm just not clear why our tutors want to spray all the new recruits in the face with this stuff. I fear we may be the butt of a sick joke. I've asked a lot of questions and the line I get back most is, 'It's voluntary but everyone does it,' to which I think, 'If it's voluntary, why would anyone do it?' It puts me in mind of YouTube clips of lads tasering each other for the LOLs except this is a bit more like Russian roulette – some people react very badly to CS gas, skin blisteringly badly. I've tried to stage a rebellion, suggesting to my fourteen classmates that we might all opt out, but the peer pressure is impossible to shift. Apparently, since this practice was introduced no one has ever refused to take part.

Until now.

At the eleventh hour, just as everyone else goes to change and get ready to head down to the car park where it's to take place, I announce to the staff that I'm out. This doesn't exactly go down a storm. Nath, one of my least favourite classmates, sneers 'Don't be a pussy.' There are a few attempts made to persuade me back into the fold but I stick to my guns – I just cannot see how knowing first-hand what being sprayed with CS gas feels like would inform my use of it in a life-or-death situation; I already know it's horrific.

Grudgingly, the course leader tells me that if I'm really not going to do it, I can carry the first-aid bag and stand on the sidelines. I hadn't counted on being made to watch – I'd hoped I could stay up in the classroom – and I feel a pang of survivor's guilt. I've saved myself but left the others behind to endure this fate. Surely that's not right?

Down in the car park, our instructors pull Darth Vader-esque gas masks on and march everyone out to the far corner, assembling my classmates into neat lines. It is an odd and oppressive scene to witness, like a mix between a firing squad and a punishment from *The Handmaid's Tale*. There has clearly been some chat about this in the staffroom as twenty or so eager sadists from the Police School, both teaching staff and trainee police officers, are huddled around the smoking area waiting to watch the spectacle. With a hiss, the aerosols are compressed and the spraying starts. Without hesitation my friends trudge unthinkingly face first into the gas as instructed.

Initially everyone looks quite relieved, smiling and laughing to each other as if they've dodged a bullet. My friend Tom, always full of puppyish silliness, playfully runs at me as if to contaminate me. I dart for shelter behind a car. He's bounding over, closing in on me, when the delayed reaction hits him. It takes twenty seconds for the effects of the gas to kick in. All at once it's carnage. People drop to the floor, others stagger and stumble in all directions or crawl on their bellies along the tarmac to cling to the wheels of parked cars, as if for dear life. It's clear none of them can see and all of them are in agony, streaming with tears as they grab and claw at their reddening faces and throats. As they scatter, the instructors try to calm the rising distress by booming, 'LOOK INTO THE WIND' (there is no wind; it's a still summer's day). 'REMEMBER, THE EFFECTS ARE TEMPORARY.'

I had no idea it would be this unpleasant. Feeling very helpless on the sidelines, I go to some of the worst hit and try to reassure them that they'll be OK.

Afterwards, they tell me it's like having crushed glass and chilli rubbed in your eyes, and that they felt suffocated, as if it was blocking their airways so that it was a struggle to breathe normally.

Before they headed down to the car park, Nath took prescription high-dose antihistamine, which has dried out his eyes, nose and throat. When activated, the CS canister sprays a jet of fibres that need moisture to react, which is why the eyes, nose and throat are usually where it hits hardest. Now he thinks he has cheated CS. Believing he's immune, he demands to be sprayed close range in the face an excessive number of times to showcase his superpower.

'Go on, spray me!'

'Spray me again!'

'And again, hahaha!'

He cackles at his defeat of the incapacitating spray. No one else cares, too engrossed in their own personal battle, but he seems drunk on some notion he is tougher than anyone in the class.

Afterwards, when my classmates have bagged up their contaminated clothes and showered carefully, he is the last to jump in the shower, smugly letting the water wash all down the front of his body, chest to crotch. The reality that it burns where it's wet must have been a rude awakening. Like trying to dowse the fire of a hot curry, only to find it spreads the effect... but so much worse. We could hear him shrieking, screaming and punching the shower-cubicle walls from outside the building.

The following morning, my friend Tom went for a swim – not something recommended within twenty-four hours of a spraying, and again the moisture reignited the CS, which burnt all over again. When we arrive in the classroom there are still bloodshot, puffy eyes and quite a few rashes and water blisters on necks to be seen. Although they look beat up, everyone unanimously expresses just how glad they are to have done it...

They didn't look glad sprawled all over the car park.

*

The Metropolitan Police Service, New Scotland Yard, is world-renowned. Greater London's police force is responsible for keeping nine million people in the UK's capital safe. Whether you're a Londoner or not, you've undoubtedly heard of the Met, perhaps read headlines and articles about work, conduct and cases undertaken by Met officers. These reports appear on a daily basis in the news. Despite all this coverage, what we hear is *about* the Met rather than *from* the Met; what happens behind the scenes remains a mystery.

In 2017, a major study of policing by Her Majesty's Inspectorate of Constabulary warned that, for the first time ever, there was a national crisis in the shortage of detectives in the Met and many other forces, placing British policing in a 'potentially perilous' state. In 2012 the number of detective vacancies in the Met was only 18; by April 2017 that figure had risen to 848. This crisis led to an unprecedented initiative: a scheme that would open the doors of Scotland Yard to a different kind of officer, ones with experience from all walks of life. These recruits would bypass time in uniform and be intensively trained as detectives before being thrown in at the deep end to learn on the job. It must have caught the public imagination: 4,500 people applied immediately. None of us had a true understanding of what the job actually involved.

I was one of the fortunate applicants that got through, one of the first 100 guinea pigs on the Metropolitan Police's new and controversial Direct Entry Detective Scheme. I felt as if I had won a golden ticket to see what crime really looks like from the frontline.

This is the story of a fascinated outsider being granted insider access, the story of how someone who binged true crime dramas late at night came to spend her days with the mad, bad and sad, confronting the darker side of humanity as her everyday reality. The Direct Entry scheme was unusual because for the first time the Met made the detective role more accessible to people of all ages without having to spend years in uniform and doing emergency response work first. And we in turn hoped to bring something different to the police force – maybe not the hardened toughness of the experienced officer who has seen it all, but a varied experience that brought other perspectives and skills from the outside world.

Was there a place for us in the Met? Could we make a difference within the system? And why, at the time of writing, have just four of our original class survived as detectives?

2
True Crime
June 2017

Let's go back a bit. It's June 2017 and I'm in a Crown Court for the first time. I'm here for a child rape trial, shadowing the barrister for the defence.

I walk into court for the first time in my life and stand still in the huge, fancy hall gazing around; it feels as if I've time-travelled, owing to the floor-to-ceiling marble and all the wigs bobbing about. Feeling out of place, I notice that the cheap jacket which I'd panic-bought first thing in an attempt to smarten me up for the occasion is already making me sweat. Helen, the barrister for the defence I'll be shadowing this week, arrives out of breath and slightly late, wearing bright red Converse, her gown billowing behind her as she comes bowling down the courtroom corridor. She flashes me a smile as she strides in. She looks atypical, yet still a force to be reckoned with. I had worried that someone dispassionate enough to try to save a paedophile from conviction might be difficult to rub along with for a week, but I like her immediately.

Within minutes, we're on our way to meet Lewis, the accused, before the trial kicks off in half an hour. I wonder what someone arrested for raping their ten-year-old stepson is going to be like? All Helen can offer me in advance of an introduction is an eye roll and a shudder.

It's such an unthinkable charge that I'm pretty shocked that he's not locked up. Instead, he has strolled into Crown Court this morning having been cooked a hearty fry-up by his mother. Lewis's mum is a timid and sweet woman who greets us warmly. Lewis is thirty-one, the same age as me.

Helen and I head into the close confines of a cupboard-sized consultation room with him. What stands out for me is that he looks so unremarkable and is calm, as if the charge he's facing is shoplifting veg from Tesco. It's odd and unsettling. He also has 'Love' and 'Hate' tattooed on his chubby knuckles, something I've never seen outside a TV drama. In real life it looks more tragic than menacing. He has the pallid, unhealthy, mild cheese-like complexion of someone who doesn't get outside much, his hair gelled greasily forward.

Lewis's line on the crime he's charged with is 'The little boy is lying.' The more time we spend with him, the more I notice that he doesn't use his name; I don't think Lewis sees his stepson as a proper person. Lewis talks a lot during these consultation sessions which, Helen tells me, is not at all the usual dynamic. Each time he tells his story he adds new details. Helen is brusque with him and doesn't entertain his theories about 'the little boy's lies'. She endlessly reminds him that adding freshly 'remembered' details at this stage will look like he's just making them up. Sitting at the edge of the room, with no clear role, I don't know how to behave and say nothing, arranging my face into a passive, slightly gormless expression. Faced with Helen's stoniness, Lewis directs the bolt-ons of his case to me, looking at me imploringly with wide eyes. He seems to think I'm buying every word.

This is the first time I've come into contact with a person charged with a serious offence, or in fact any criminal offence, and I'm curious and intrigued. Perhaps it is the contrast with the security of my own background, but I'm fascinated by the people who commit these incomprehensible crimes, what makes them do the things they do. And by the process of bringing them to justice – how the evidence is amassed to secure the conviction.

Over four days, I watch the case unfold, much like a member of the jury, except that I am actually sitting behind the suspect. In fact, many of the jury glower at me, assuming that I must be on Lewis's side, perhaps his loyal but deluded girlfriend. But I am also privy to the out-of-trial sessions where the defence and prosecution barristers and the judge debate points of law and the arrangement of the trial. I had always imagined the defence and the prosecution would be intensely locked in head-to-head combat. Instead, the biggest lesson I learn about criminal barristers is that it's really not about winning. Both sides play their part and present the evidence on behalf of their client, with the judge as the referee so that the jury can make their decision based on the facts of the case. Winning or losing is irrelevant, it's justice prevailing that is important.

Nor are defence barristers devoid of morals as I'd assumed. They have no choice in who they do or don't represent, getting handed their client by cab-rank system, based on who's available and next in line. While the accused is in court it is the barrister's job to be his or her mouthpiece. There is no collusion or coaching behind closed doors to work out how to worm their client out of the charges against them, and they get paid for their time in court either way.

By the end of day one, I'm convinced that Lewis is guilty. We've been shown a video interview with Otis, the victim. He's ten years old, with scrappily pulled-back hair and full of fidgety energy, unable to sit still and going off on random tangents just like any little kid. When the interviewer gently brings him back on track, the interview centres on his stepdad, our Lewis – him showing porn, his erection, asking his stepson to 'wink' him off and putting something in his bottom. The boy knows what Lewis did to him is odd, but he doesn't yet realise the extent of the violation as he trusts Lewis. He's been groomed. Besides, Lewis's told him not to tell his mum, brother or sister, 'otherwise you'll get taken away'.

In the interview the detective is amazing. You can hear her voice off camera, kindly and calmly asking the little boy what happened, subtly probing to bring out the facts but without asking leading questions or re-traumatising a child who has already been through something no child should experience. She's poised and professional in court. I can't stop thinking about the significance of what she's done. Without her painstakingly assembling the evidence there would be no case: from the moment Otis spoke up – he told his granny – this detective had worked to bring this case to trial. Without her work, Lewis's crimes would have gone on, catastrophically unchecked.

The facts themselves are often hard to take. That afternoon we hear that Lewis's DNA matched semen that was found on a bed sheet taken from the boy's little bed, exactly where he had said the sexual assault happened in his bedroom. One of the jury members looks like she's about to throw up.

At the end of the day, Helen and I meet with Lewis again and in the wake of all the damning evidence he is as chilled as he was that morning. Unphased, he sets about explaining away everything we heard. The thing about being guilty but claiming you're not, is that if you're not careful the account you give will descend into farce. It's all but impossible to pass off a fleshed-out lie as the truth when forensic links, amongst other evidence, are stacked against you.

Day four, the final day of the trial, is Lewis's time in the box. Aside from the fact that his stepson has painted a distressingly vivid picture of things that should be far beyond the realms of a child's imagination, Lewis has to explain away being forensically linked to a kid's bed and explain how he was able to talk about his sexual exploits. It's fair to say Lewis has his work cut out for him. He gives his account, before being mercilessly cross-examined.

He tells the jury that he got bored of 'wanking' in the bathroom and so decided to do it in another room instead… a child's bedroom. He claims Otis had known he'd 'jizzed' on his bed as he'd hidden a camera in his room to see if people came in, because he was annoyed with his siblings going in without permission. The judge intervenes at this point, to ask why Lewis would go and masturbate in there, when he knew the boy was filming? Quick as a flash Lewis tries to defend his actions by explaining he had 'checked the room and he wasn't filming that day'. In that one reply Lewis undermines his entire story. There are gasps from the jury as his web of lies is ripped apart by this one well-aimed question. Lewis has tied himself in knots before hanging himself with his own rope.

The jury withdraws. An hour later they reach a verdict, just as Lewis saunters back in from his roast lunch.

His casualness is remarkable. There is no anxiety I've experienced quite like that which rises up as a jury filters back into a court-room, their minds made up and about to give their verdict. I can feel the tension coursing through me. A flicker of panic comes over me: would they believe his lies? Or believe beyond reasonable doubt that he committed the offences? Could he walk free? This feels like the ultimate cliff-hanger, but this is real life and this ver-dict has a life-changing impact.

He is found guilty on all counts. The judge closes the trial by saying she has found him to be a callous and barefaced liar who has shown no remorse for the appalling things he's done. She states that it's her belief this was the start of what would have been an ongoing campaign of hideous abuse. She finishes by saying she will sentence him in a month, that she won't be lenient with that sentence and that until then he'll be remanded in custody. With that she booms 'Take him down!' and he is escorted down the stairs within the dock directly to the cells in the bowels of the building.

On the way down to the cells where Lewis has been taken, we see his mum, who thanks Helen for her professionalism. I realise that she knows her son did these unthinkable things, but she stood by him anyway. Such is a mother's love.

The cells under this crown court are so old, damp and grim, quite the stark contrast to all the grandeur upstairs. Doors slam, chains clink and we're shown into a cell with green peeling paint on the walls and a burly uniformed guard at the door. For the first time Lewis is rattled – his leg is twitching relentlessly – and says that he wants to appeal. 'Too late,' Helen tells him bluntly. 'You can't appeal a jury's verdict, that's not how it works.' I pity him in this moment of hopelessness, as he sits there in this gross cell stripped of his liberty. His forthcoming imprisonment – fif-teen years for raping a minor, and a lifetime on the sex-offenders register – while no less than he deserves, is unimaginable to me. But Otis and his siblings are now safe.

As for me, I've never felt a buzz like it. The theatre of it all, my fascination with the criminal, my sympathy for the victim, the suspense of the verdict, but most of all the significance. I have a soaring feeling that I love the drama of court, of seeing justice in action.

Outside the court, there is an exhausted but jubilant feeling of congratulation, of a job well done. Helen and I go to thank the detective.

'You were great,' I blurt out like a fangirl.

She looks me up and down. 'You must be a baby barrister.'

'I wish. I'd love to do what you do and be a part of this.'

'You actually can. The Met's on the cusp of launching a scheme that lets people apply straight to detective.'

'Really?!'

'Yeah, you should look it up. Direct Entry Detective, it's called. Fast track. I've got to warn you though, it's controversial. Some in the job very vocally say you can't be a real police officer if you skip time in uniform. Not me though. I'm for it, bringing more people in. And God knows, there's more than enough work to go around.'

This whole week, as I've grown increasingly enamoured with criminal justice, I've been calculating the logistics and cost of retraining to become a barrister. Training takes two years, and would cost me £30,000, not to mention the loss of any income and the cost of living for that time. Almost a six-figure sum of money I didn't have. Her revelation about this new scheme is the lightbulb moment, the solution I've been searching for. A detective is the heavyweight when it comes to criminal proceedings; barristers show up for court and major in the endgame. All the substance of the case is the work of detectives. Without their investigations there would never be another charge, trial or conviction in this country.

The next day, I'm on the Tube, leafing through a discarded copy of *Metro*, when I see the scheme advertised. The words 'THIS COULD BE YOUR FIRST MAJOR BREAKTHROUGH' are emblazoned on a dark background. 'Crime is changing and so is the way the Met recruits.' The advert is illustrated with an evidence bag emblazoned with the words 'You can now join as a detective constable'. The entry wage is not lavish – £30,000 for a job in central London – but its draw isn't the money. The thought that I could be working on real-life cases within months blows my mind. No years in uniform, no pounding the streets as a police constable; instead, a twenty-week fast-track training and then on to the job investigating the worst crime in London.

It feels like one of those signs from the universe – when you encounter something new to you and then suddenly you see and hear about it everywhere you go. I've already decided I'll apply, and later that day I fill in the forms, and press submit. I don't overthink it, I don't debate the opportunity with friends and family, I just do it. It feels like such a moonshot, I don't think I'll stand a chance of going the distance and actually getting the job.

3

Lost but Chasing the Dream

If I had to choose a word to describe my life when I applied for the Met, it would be 'chasing'. Chasing the pieces of the puzzle that would make my somewhat messy and chaotic life all come together.

My unconventional week of work experience in my thirties with Helen at a Crown Court came as I was trying to find my next step. I was living out of bags between my parents' house and my boyfriend's, and I was working, as I did when I was between jobs, for my friend Tom, as part of his care team.

Tom and I have known each other since we were babies, and have been great family friends ever since. We grew up living parallel lives but when he was fifteen a brain tumour and subsequent catastrophic bleed changed that. While still as sharp as ever, Tom now faces challenges with aspects of life so many of us take for granted.

I would do two twelve-hour night shifts back to back each week, 8 p.m. to 8 a.m., taking the National Express coach for two hours first and napping en route, and then snatching a further forty-five-minute power nap in my regular bedroom at Tom's parents' house. Tom and I would hang out and watch TV series and films together; he arguably has a more refined taste in these than I. When Tom went to bed at midnight I would sit alone on the squishy leather sofa in the kitchen watching endless true crime by lamplight, the tackier the better as the night went on. Sometimes Tom wouldn't go to bed but instead a group of us would take a trip to London for a minimal techno all-night rave. Preferring the calm nights playing sofa sleuth to being in the packed club stone-cold sober, I would meditate my way through. I earned the nickname 'the fun sponge' for suggesting we leave the party before 6 a.m.

Wherever we were, at home, in the club or – the ultimate highlight – on the coast in the South of France for the annual family holiday, it never felt like work, more like hanging out with a lifelong friend.

Ten years earlier I'd graduated from Durham University with a perfectly decent, perfectly useless degree in Ancient History and French. I remember, the summer we graduated, my best friend had a twenty-first birthday party in her garden. The collision of the words 'garden' and 'party' make us sound privileged, and I suppose we were. I'd had a sheltered upbringing in rural Cheshire. My dad had grafted to give us the great education that he'd never had; my mum stayed at home to look after me and my brothers whilst we were young. I'd mostly sailed through school – good at exams, good at making friends – without any more than the usual adolescent drama. I'd been to the same school from four to eighteen. Most of the friends around me, I'd known since we were tiny, and now we had graduated, full of ambition, energy and enthusiasm, ready to be challenged, useful and expecting to be successful.

My friend's dad got up to make a speech at the party – the usual heartfelt toast, but with a rueful sign-off about the state of the global economy. We raised our glasses to the immortal line 'You're all fucked.' We laughed. It didn't dampen our spirits; we knew no different or better.

Off I went, into my twenties, full of aimless ambition. I tried all the jobs true to the millennial stereotype. First stop: management consultant, a six-month contract, a good graduate job. Well paid, working in risk management with DEFRA and some government agencies, but based at home. Boredom set in pretty quick.

I finished the contract, then took off to work in Australia for a year and afterwards travelled the well-worn backpacker route through New Zealand, Asia and even southern Africa. Home again: next stop, advertising. Further stops along the way: research, strategy, sales. I could never quite buy into the line that you had stick at something for two years for the CV before you quit. If I felt 'No!' it was time to move on. I was chasing the elusive goal – a job I enjoyed and believed in, that stretched me, with people I liked, that paid me enough to live well in London. Was that too much to ask? It would appear so.

I had arrived in London in 2012, this time for a low-paid internship with an advertising agency, another six-month contract, but with the promise of a permanent job at the end were I to prove myself of value. I recall feeling like an excited adventurer taking my first intrepid step: this was professional life in the bright lights of the big city. With no job certainty, I started out sharing a double bed with my best friend in her bedroom and splitting her rent down the middle. So what? It was fun and reminded me of our time away travelling and all the makeshift sleeping arrangements we'd endured as we made our way through South-East Asia and southern Africa, becoming increasingly resourceful as our budget dwindled. I remember one time we even shared a bowl of soup for lunch, we were that broke. I was cool with the chaotic living and the roughing it that went with it and besides, it was temporary. At least, that was my plan.

I loved London, the buzz of it, my friends and social life, but felt like I had never quite cracked it. Maybe that was what kept me there – the thought that one day I might make it. But as the years rolled by, I seemed to survive from a bulging suitcase in one friend's spare room or another's. Years spent living somewhere in the realms of mate's rates and sofa surfing, interspersed with living with boyfriends out of convenience.

The main, misguided focus of my twenties was finding 'the one'. I was a romantic and that made me a serial monogamist. I suppose because Mum and Dad are such a great team, I always felt that the relationship was the most important thing, often to the detriment of everything else. I didn't go for a particular type of person – unless complicated is a type – but each time I would just throw myself in wholeheartedly, all or nothing. Not necessarily learning from past mistakes but full of optimism and hope that it would go the distance.

Then, the year before applying to the Met, I had met Josh. We had spent the best year of my life together. I adored him. He was funny – we laughed constantly – and smart, brilliant, eccentric, creative, had the sexiest voice I think I've ever heard, gorgeous… I could go on and on. Being with him enriched my life like never before. He was an introvert to my extrovert. Josh was five years older than me, and after his own years of searching for the right path, had set up a start-up, an energy switching company. It was going well with him, but we hadn't quite settled. We couldn't agree on the terms on which I should move into his flat, and we couldn't seem to resolve it.

Transience that was fun in my twenties had now become tainted with despair in my thirties. Most of my friends had settled to some extent. Friends from school had returned to Cheshire and now had houses, husbands and at least two kids. Even my friends in London, while they might not have settled down or even bought a house, so impossible were the property prices, had mostly settled on an industry. Although I wasn't envious of them and didn't feel left behind, I felt like I had never joined the race in the first place.

The truth was, I'd always done things my own way and on my own timeline. My years since graduation, while they hadn't yielded a straightforward career path, had taught me things about myself. I was resilient. I'm slight and quite delicate to look at, so people tend to assume I have no fight in me. But from job to job, and relationship to relationship, I picked myself up and kept going. I'd bounce and bounce and bounce, never down for long, always believing in the next thing. When Josh had his time of feeling directionless he had really panicked; I always took the view that things would turn out right. I was happy-go-lucky, and always saw the lighter side of life.

I had a high threshold for risk and adventure. My line was, if it wasn't going to kill me, why not try it? What was the worst that could happen? Sure, I wasn't as devil-may-care as I'd been at twenty-two – these days I'd dropped trying anything that might mean my parents getting a terrible phone call and I wasn't about to go and live in a treehouse in Bali selling timeshare again. But I was, for lack of a better word, ballsy. I wasn't easily phased.

And I had tenacity and a strong sense of justice. One job in particular had made me realise this and just how much fairness and integrity mattered to me.

In 2015 I came back from Bali, full of business ideas but empty of cash, and took a job in sales with a huge tech company, hoping the commission might offer me financial freedom one day. It was a young company – just five years old, so technically a start-up – and the staff were young too, median age twenty-five. Everyone was fun and good-looking, and business was booming. The office – a huge open place on the north bank of the Thames – virtually screamed 'work hard, play hard, guys!' Everything was bright orange, from the carpets to the beanbags and ping-pong table, to the funky merch given to the most influential members of staff. As someone who had thrived on the camaraderie of school, I immediately loved the sociability and the feeling of being part of the gang.

And what a gang we were. I'd joined in the summer: my introductory drinks and every subsequent bi-weekly summer session took place on the riverside. As the season changed, we moved into what was known as 'the bat cave', a dingy underground pub, where each time we would swear we would just go for one, but would end up buying rounds by the bottle of cheap wine to lube up for karaoke led by DJ Dave with his laminated folder of tunes, tiny biros and paper request slips. I'll sing anything in a crowd for a crowd as long as it's a banger of a tune (my go-to is Westlife's 'You Raise Me Up' – make of that what you will).

The work was good too. I buzzed in the morning as I strode across London Bridge getting high on the best Thameside views of London, a colourful little figure in jeans springing along in the sea of commuters in their dark suits and overcoats. The company was a marketing platform which offered deals for subscribers to sample produce, services and experiences offered by local businesses at a discounted price in return for a hulking cut of, if not all of, the profit from any ensuing sales. I was on the Inbound team, a low-paid temporary holding pen where all new recruits started out, a rite of passage before graduating to become a 'hunter' (wrangler of new business) or a 'farmer' (account manager) where you started to get a real taste of the profit you made for the company.

After six months I'd done my time on Inbound. By now I'd seen a few guys who'd joined at the same time as me get headhunted onto the other teams without interview – one day they were sitting in our team, the next they were springboarded across the office – but this hadn't happened to me. So that November I sent my sales figures to the manager of a 'hunting' team, HR sent me a date for an internal interview and I got the job based on perform-ance. I would become the second girl on the team commencing in January. That was that, and I was thrilled.

Except, in the week before Christmas, things unravelled at an alarming rate. The day after I met my new boss to firm up the details of my new role, my old boss announced that I couldn't be released from his team. Confused, I contacted HR, but before they could get back to me, he told me that it was his team or nothing. When I questioned this and told him I'd involved HR, he said, 'I didn't want to have to do this, sweetheart, but you're fired.' And just like that I was a casualty of an Alan Sugar TV-style firing, so my new job became no job.

The next day, despite assurances from HR that he couldn't just fire me on the spot, without notice, no previous disciplinary issue and only a good performance track record, I was called back in and fired again, retrospectively, this time following a semblance of procedure. Like so many others before and after me, I was disposed of. A sloppy clean-up job on his and HR's part, no legal recourse on mine.

Perhaps I was naive, but I was stunned by the injustice of it. I just could not believe that anyone could do this, and was horrified by the complicity of the organisation and my absolute impo-tence in the face of it. A couple of friends wanted there to be more to the story, something else I did or said to provoke what happened – the idea of the big successful company treating a lowly employee badly seemed to make them feel uneasy about their own workplace security. In the days, weeks and months that followed, almost everyone (except my Dad, who was a rock) told me to move on. It happens all the time, they told me, much better for you to leave it be, it's bad but there's nothing you can do about it. Former colleagues, including my friend Olie, tried to comfort me saying 'they're dogs, they've done it to tons and tons of people'. Yet the fact that it happened all the time made it, if anything, worse. I couldn't reconcile myself to any workplace being like the Wild West.

I was raging and couldn't seem to let it go. I had loved this job, so first I tried to appeal to the powers that be at the company and when that didn't work out, I wanted justice, not just for myself but so that it couldn't happen to other people. I went at it, like a dog with the proverbial bone. I read everything in an effort to demystify employment law and tribunals. I went to legal drop-in centres at local libraries to speak with lawyers, roped in friends and family who worked in any vague legal capacity, and made phone calls to the Citizens Advice Bureau. I was obstructed by the fact that it was going to cost more than £1,000 to bring my case to an employment tribunal, not including legal fees. I couldn't afford that: I had been low paid and now I was unemployed, picking up occasional shifts with Tom.

Also, there was a huge loophole in employment law. An employee could only bring a claim of unfair dismissal if they had worked for the employer for two years. Knowing that we live in a world where people change job frequently, and this is even more true of low-paid jobs, made me even more indignant. A huge proportion of the workplace was as vulnerable as I had been.

For two and a half years I continued to seek some kind of recompense. And when, in July 2017, Unison, one of the major trade unions, won a landmark victory in the Supreme Court ruling that employment tribunal fees were unlawful and unconstitutional and must be scrapped immediately, the triumph felt both systemic and personal. I filed my case immediately.

But for me, it turned out that this process had done something that lasted a lot longer than the job and subsequent battle. It had identified my drive: I realised that caring that something is wrong, and trying to put that right, gives me a sense of purpose. It lights a kind of fire in me. I could see that this was what I needed from a job.

So when I heard about the Direct Entry scheme, it felt like the answer – not just for a career path, and a next step, but for work that mattered. I had a friend who was in the police force and it had never appealed – the thought of being in physical conflict or using force on members of the public wasn't for me. But a detective? The detective in court had changed the course of that little girl's life. This was a job where I could help to right wrongs.

4

Pressure Test

Summer 2017

I'm scurrying across an unfamiliar part of west London. I've no difficulty heading for my destination — thirty storeys of glass and concrete, with a distinctive curved hourglass shape, the Empress State Building towers over everything around it. I feel like I'm about to climb aboard a spaceship, and not only because the tasks that lie ahead of me at today's assessment centre feel utterly alien.

I've already spent a Saturday on a preparation course for what lies ahead. I received a thick pack in the post with information, including a list of thirty or forty competencies the Met are looking for and a map of a fictional shopping centre, along with details of its management structure and policies. But while I've been prepared, I don't feel in any way ready.

On arrival I'm led to a waiting section of the vast atrium where there must be a couple of hundred people milling about. As I look around me, I struggle to discern a target applicant — the people I'm surrounded by are anything from twenty-five to sixty, from every kind of background. It's as if the scheme has flung the Met wide open.

We're all wearing large stickers displaying our candidate numbers, although for some reason mine is the only one that's handwritten in biro. It looks like I've made my own badge and sneaked in, or perhaps that's my imposter syndrome talking. As we wait, the silence among us becomes oppressive, so I go for an easy opener, and ask the people nearest to me, 'Did you go to the interview preparation day?'

All the girls and a couple of men say yes or nod, but all the white guys look confused. 'What interview prep thing?' one of them responds.

I recall noticing that there was a disproportionate amount of women at the preparation day, and now that I come to think of it, the men there weren't white, but now I realise that we were being given a targeted leg-up, white men were not invited to the session. Writing in 2022, BAME officers only make up 7.3 per cent of the Met, which nowhere near reflects the fact that 40 per cent of London's population are from Asian, Black, Mixed and other ethnic backgrounds. Women in the Met (29.9 per cent of officers) are the lowest numbers of any force in England and Wales.

The Met needs more diversity, however I don't believe using positive discrimination is a fair way to achieve that goal. Speaking as a woman, righting what's been unfair and historically a male dominated institution by offering an unfair advantage, far from providing a quick fix to make the numbers go in the right direc-tion, is overcorrection which hurts the cause by further polarising, breeding resentment and undermining the very foundation of fair treatment needed for equality. Even if, at surface level, the numbers tally.

A group of about thirty of us have our names called and are taken up to the twenty-third floor and into a classroom that serves as a holding pen. Maybe if I stay in the process long enough I'll make it to the Orbit, the state-of-the-art revolving glass restaurant on the thirtieth floor. Here we wait in silence, the calm before the storm.

Names are called out four at a time and those that leave never return to the room. To soothe my nerves, I've been chanting the Met core values on a loop in my head: Professionalism, Integrity,

Courage, Compassion. Professionalism, Integrity, Courage, Compassion. Professionalism, Integrity, Courage, Compassion…

'Jessica McDonald …' I'm up.

Outside in the corridor, we're told what's going to happen next. We'll be doing a series of four role-play assessments with actors in separate rooms, rotating around them one at a time. When the klaxon sounds we've got to stop what we are doing and will be led to the next stage. This is the pressure test I've been told about.

First, we're shown to a desk with reading material on it. When the klaxon sounds we have to read and digest said material. After five minutes the klaxon will sound again, which signals that we have to stop and step away from the desk. We'll be escorted to a doorway and, when another klaxon sounds, enter and 'deal with what awaits'. Five minutes later, klaxon, we will leave the room we're in, get to a new desk, klaxon… We are to undergo this process four times, entering a different mystery room each time.

If it sounds like *The Crystal Maze*, it is. The whole day is. We need to get through this round to be allowed through to the next heat of the recruitment process.

I sit down at the first desk and try to assimilate the huge stack of paperwork. There is a LOT and it's cryptic: email chains, corporate structures, contracts, newspaper articles, names, dates, incidents. It's all linked to a complaint about a boy in a shopping centre of which, for the purpose of the exercise, I'm acting manager. WTF. Piecing together the story, it seems the nursery manager believes this boy is a threat to the children. Another document tells me that the boy has autism and is also obsessed with trains.

Where to start? The klaxon honks me out of desperate cram mode and off I stumble to my first doorway, head swimming and drunk on information. I enter, and no sooner have I set foot across the threshold, than I am in the role play. 'I WANT MARTIN YOUNG BANNED FROM THIS SHOPPING CENTRE!' an irate woman, red-faced and eyes popping, yells at me, smacking the desk as she delivers her line. The actor is very dramatic and convincing – this is her moment. I know from my frantic reading that Martin Young is the autistic boy I'd learnt about. And off we go. My job is to investigate and work out what each person in each room is upset about, find out the root cause, and what they want, and then try to calm and defuse this confrontation situation pragmatically – and quickly. In what seems like no time the klaxon goes: another situation, another confrontation. Spoiler alert: they're all raging. There is a silent assessor in the corner of each room observing and rating the interaction.

I learn quickly that you can't win these people over – these actors have been briefed to stay furious, no matter what's said to them. It's about good communication, de-escalation of a conflict situation and keeping your cool when your first, second and third efforts to calm them don't work.

But what's really hard is switching from one intense experience to the next. After the first room I eat into a big chunk of my reading time in advance of the next gauntlet replaying the previous encounter in my head and regretting the fact that I didn't even bother to introduce myself. I just stood there stunned, taking a dog's abuse. Shit. Time's ticking past. I need to read.

Read, room, read, room, read, room, read, room, done.

By the end of this test my brain feels like mush and I can't hold my train of thought any more. As with any exam or test I've ever done I only remember the low points: in one room I became so conscious of slipping up and causing offence to a disabled customer that I referred to wheelchairs as 'mobility chariots' as I overcompensated, dancing on eggshells and desperate to provoke no further negative reaction. In another, the owner of a bridal shop apparently hated me on sight and took offence at every word I said. In that first room, it took everything to not yell, 'HE WASN'T STARING AT THE LITTLE KIDS!' Every scenario we encountered had information that we knew but couldn't disclose – something that meant we couldn't just back down but had to show some backbone, pushing back against unreasonable and sometimes outrageous requests.

Next comes the Maths test. It has been years since I've done more than add up a restaurant bill – I feel sure I've failed it. Then literacy. I'm left-handed and have always found writing by hand slow and laborious, and do not finish the paper.

The day is not going seamlessly – for me, or for the organisers. There is no time for lunch and a lot of waiting around. I guess there must be a hundred applicants being sifted today, and we are all rotating around the various tasks involved in the selection. It's not surprising it's a shambles.

In the medical I am caught off guard when I am told I need to have a handful of my hair chopped off for a drugs test. A mere 200 strands, I'm told, but it sounds a lot, especially when I'd thought I'd just have to wee in a pot. With that, a substantial chunk of hair was lopped off dead centre at the back, an inch from the root. I leave with a new tuft, and a headful of unanswered questions about how they harvest the hair from someone with a shaved head.

The wait for the hearing test becomes bottle-necked. I sit for two hours waiting to be seen and meet a woman also going for the job, who used to work on Crimewatch, the TV show. She's forthright and sparky, one of those rare people who light up a room; they should definitely pick her, I think. She also whispers that she has five children but tells me not to tell anyone.

Finally I'm called, ushered into a soundproof box, handed padded headphones and told to press a handheld button every time I hear the beep. It's dark in here and I crush my eyes closed as if this helps me concentrate even more on the sound as the pitch and frequency change. It's all going fine until the pitch gets extremely high and suddenly the beep is gone, and doesn't come back. And, having held it together all day, I start to panic.

The beep's still gone. It's been gone for ages now. Oh God, I think. I'm deaf. I won't get the job now and I've got deafness to contend with too. I've always known my hearing isn't all that good (I blame it on the fact that I have tiny mouse-like ears). Tears prick my eyes. And as I sit in the darkness and see my chances diminishing from something outside my control, I realise I really, really want this job.

Every situation has called on me to use everything I've got, to be fully present, and use all my wits. The more it demands of me, the more I want it. There's none of the boredom I've felt in office jobs. I've loved the pressure and intensity of the situations. Running the gauntlet of challenges of the day, needing to question, piece things together and get the story out of people feels like it's made for me. As I sit in the darkness it dawns on me that getting through this day means everything to me. Then I hear the beep again, it's dropped back into my range.

The door of the box opens and the technician peers in, 'All right in there?!' she asks sweetly. 'Your hearing is fine. Just head back to the waiting area and you'll be called for the next test.' As I skip to the waiting area, I feel like I've just got my life back.

Next up is blood pressure. After no lunch, crashing blood sugar and the hysteria of being hard of hearing, it's higher than it should be. I'm told I've failed the test. The nurse tells me that it's gone so high that I can't continue with the interviewing process. This news does not bring it down any. I beg her to take it one more time and, seeing my desperation, she does, out of kindness. This time, she tells me to lean back and close my eyes. 'Pretend you're on the beach. The sand beneath your feet, the warmth of the sun on your face, the sound of the tide washing in on the shore...' Instead I recall Commissioner Cressida Dick saying in an interview that she was thankful to a similarly kind staff member who measured her height generously when she joined the Met as she fell just below their entrance requirements.

Whatever I think, it works, and my blood pressure is down. Eight hours after I entered, I stagger out of the building into daylight, the golden hour, feeling as if it should be midnight.

*

A couple of months later and we're back for the second day of assessments: interview day. I have made it through the first round, have completed a not very challenging fitness test, and now we, the crowd of increasingly hopefuls, have assembled for our one-on-ones. This is the chance to explain what makes us suited for this role and what we can bring to it. I look around to see if I recognise anyone from the previous session, but that day was such a blur of rotating tasks, and there are still so many candidates, that no one stands out. I hope the woman with the five children got through.

Giving up on facial recognition, I look at what we're all wearing. We've gone for an interesting array of outfits in a bid to 'dress for the job you want' – but none of us truly knows what a detective wears day to day. There's a sensible crew who've gone for no-frills standard corporate dress and wouldn't look out of place in a sleek city law firm. A fair few women are in a power trouser suit in black or blue with an ugly pair of black clompy shoes. Then there's another gaggle who seem to have decided this look might be too polished and have gone for a grittier alternative, fascinating variations on a generic TV-detective-inspired look. They've stopped short of deerstalker hats and a magnifying glass, but there is an abundance of trench coats. Long hair has been scraped back. A few girls have opted for a severe bun complete with hairnet that puts me in mind of the cold meat counter at the supermarket. There is a total absence of skirts and dresses. I'm wearing a polka-dot dress, which looked conservative when I put it on this morning, but now sticks out a mile.

I feel OK about this day. I relish a job interview. On paper my meandering career path and gap-ridden CV isn't impressive by any stretch. But people are so much more than a chronological list of spun professional achievement. The interview is the time to build that rapport and get across who you are and the experience you've had. Maybe it's years of having to think on my feet in sales jobs, but I feel ready for what I think they might throw at me.

This interview is different, though. It starts normally enough; I'm ushered into the room by an interviewer who smiles but doesn't introduce herself, which I think is in the interest of fairness; we're a number in this process rather than a named person. Once I'm seated she explains the format of the interview. I will be asked a question and then given five uninterrupted minutes to answer it. The question will also be placed in front of me in enormous Times New Roman print on a laminated sheet of A4. She's got a stopwatch to monitor the response time. First question: 'What is the importance of community?'

'In the context of policing?' I ask.

She gives no answer but shunts the laminated sheet a little closer to me. I start confidently enough, talking about policing within the community, and the importance of mutual respect and trust, of working together, about the different communities within London, but thirty seconds in, I'm rambling. I look at her; her face is impassive. Not one single minimal encourager. I go on, waiting to be challenged or for one of my points to land, but it's like talking to a wall. On and on, just me, monologuing away. I hate giving a monologue. I'd prepared for a rally and the back-and-forth volley of question and answer, but this is gruelling. Eventually I falter to a close. 'So um, yeah, community and how we interact with community is of utmost importance...'

She says, 'You still have eighty-two seconds on the clock if there is anything more you'd like to add,' but I've said more than enough.

All of the questions centre around those key Met values: Professionalism, Integrity, Courage and Compassion, plus some additional criteria they've decided we need to have on top of those; adaptability and resilience seem to be key. At one point I start talking about working for Tom. Tom's situation usually evokes compassion in even the hardest heart, but this time I see nothing, not even a flicker in her eyes. Everything I'd banked on, making a connection, finding common ground, doesn't work here. I'm so desperate to make her react, I can hardly remember what I'm talking about. Briefly a scene from 24 Hours in Police Custody flashes into my head – the detectives vainly questioning a man who responds to everything with a blank 'no comment'. It's so awkward, is this what it will be like?

Then we're done. The stonewalling is over. She relaxes and asks me some interested and engaged questions about some of the things I'd said for the last few minutes, and we have a lovely easy chat.

Next, the worst interview I've ever had is swiftly followed by the in-tray exercise. This time I'm playing a police role – I'm covering for my boss and I have to draw up a table of my boss's caseload in order of priority. Different cases have different timings, urgency and levels of severity. We have to analyse the factors involved – vulnerable adults, children, old people, jobs that are far away, jobs with higher and lower levels of risk to others and officers alike.

I've drawn my table and am filling it in when different notifications come in, then there are interruptions – multiple updates about situation changes; someone walking into the room saying 'We've just heard there's been a stabbing round the corner', which shunts items down the list; new items have to be written into my timetable in tiny biro rows. By the time I'm finished my table is a mess of arrows and asterisks and additions. I'm then taken to present this plan in person to a senior ranking police officer, who grills me on my rationale.

Compared to this, the late afternoon panel interview falls away in my memory. I can scarcely remember what they asked me about, only that adrenalin got me through the day.

It's hard, after jumping through all those hoops, to go back to normal life. I decide to try and visualise the future I want to see, and to help me I order a copy of *Blackstone's Criminal Practice*, a £70 monster of a book, the girth of two stacked copies of the Yellow Pages with about as much narrative excitement. This book forms the syllabus for the National Detective Exam, which, I hold out a tiny shoot of hope, I ought to be sitting in a matter of months if I get the job. Instead, it looks at me reproachfully as it works its magic as a doorstop in my childhood bedroom when I spend patches of time at my parents'.

So when, in October – Halloween to be precise – three months after I'd applied, I open an email telling me I'm in, I'm over-the-moon happy. I can picture where and when I was at that moment. I was helping a friend by covering her nannying job for the month (while she went to pick weed in California), working with a lovely family in Essex. The little girls I was looking after had dressed me up as the witch, Elphaba from *Wicked*, and I was sitting, body painted green on all visible skin, in the local pub in the aftermath of the pumpkin-carving competition. I was so elated that I told everyone and anyone my news. I'd like to bottle that feeling of sheer joy for ever. It felt like the solution to everything, in a way that just a few months before I couldn't have even imagined.

Finally, I thought, finally it has all come good.

5

Limbo

Autumn 2017

The job is mine, subject to enhanced vetting clearance, start date TBC. I rush to fill in the additional information needed and send it all off sharpish, then call the contact number to ask how long vetting will take and when the start date is likely to be. At the end of the phone is Bryn, a highly personable and jolly Welshman. He says it can take two weeks but up to six. 'As soon as it clears we'll get you the next available start date. There will be one intake a month,' he says.

But this is just the start of Bryn's and my enduring relationship. Vetting doesn't take two weeks or even six. Six weeks drifts into six months, during which I call Bryn more than I call my closest friends or my parents. Bryn, friendly as he is, can't offer me any more information than he gave me that first day we spoke. It appears the vetting staff (judging by their pace there can be only a few) service the entire country from a bunker buried deep underground, totally cut off from the world. I imagine them surrounded by floor-to-ceiling piles of toppling forms. In my mind they wear black, grim reaper-style robes and communicate by carrier pigeon or smoke signal. How else to explain how long it is taking? Too few people doing too much work and the impact on the speed of things progressing is a reality that will become a theme in the Met.

The longer I wait, the more paranoid I become that I won't get clearance. The vetting process looks into my past and that of my immediate family and partner. As far as I know we're blameless (although I do start wondering what skeletons my angelic Catholic mother, who claims to have only got drunk once in her life, could possibly have in the cupboard) but a seemingly innocuous part of my own past might be difficult: my previous addresses. One of the eligibility criteria for the Met is that candidates must have lived in London for three years. We have to provide a list of previous addresses from the past seven years. I've been in London since 2012 so you'd think this would be a quick green tick in the box. But those years, with their rackety accommodation set-ups, never staying anywhere longer than six months, and living with similarly transient flatmates, are hard to keep track of. If I were to create an infographic highlighting where I've stayed and the duration on a map of London, there would be a swathe of little dots peppering the town. To this day the majority of my post is sent to my parents' house in Cheshire.

I go to visit Josh in San Francisco. He's been based in California for the past few months and I've missed him. He has just shy of six months to go as he's won a place at the top Silicon Valley start-up accelerator. He's smashing it, living every tech entrepreneur's dream. Even though I couldn't be prouder, I have moments when I feel sorry for myself as the career I badly want to start is just out of reach. Still, Josh himself, and the exploration of that incredible city and its surrounding countryside under cobalt blue skies, calm my nerves. When I'm with him I am perfectly content, there is no one I'd rather be with and nowhere I'd rather be.

I suck up the agony of limbo. Until one day, for the very first time in half a year, ten months after I first applied to the scheme, Bryn makes his first and only outbound call to me. I'm vetted and clear. I really do start in two weeks.

6

Back to School

Spring–Summer 2018

I, Jessica McDonald, of the Metropolitan Police Service
do solemnly and sincerely declare and affirm
that I will well and truly serve the Queen in the office of
constable,
with fairness, integrity, diligence and impartiality.
Upholding fundamental human rights
and according equal respect to all people.
And that I will,
to the best of my power,
cause the peace to be kept and preserved,
and prevent all offences against people and property;
and that while I continue to hold said office,
I will to the best of my skill and knowledge
discharge all duties thereof faithfully according to law.

It's official, I'm a sworn-in police officer and have signed the
Official Secrets Act.

Day one, and we, the thirty new recruits of the Direct Entry
scheme, join every other new police constable in the 600-seat
auditorium at Hendon, the Metropolitan Police Training Centre.

As we filter to our assigned seats the massive screen in front of us reads: 'THE BEST JOB IN THE WORLD'.

Arriving at Hendon you certainly feel it – the glass, the security barriers and staff who man them, the many floors we're not permitted to access, the sense that you might rub shoulders with anyone from a chief superintendent to the Commissioner. It is only us awestruck new recruits who gather round the glass cabinet housing the eternal flame that burns for all those who have fallen in the line of duty – everyone else bristles with purpose as they stride past. For now we are only allowed on the ground and first floors. We have all been issued with photo passes, which we must wear visibly at all times in the building but never outside. I only hope this isn't going to be used for my official Police Warrant Card ('the badge') – I look like an absolute simpleton.

We sit through two days of induction, equal parts terrifying and mind-numbing. Pension schemes, healthcare options, insurance, critical illness cover, even a chance to buy into the legendary 'Goring', where for a monthly debit off your pay packet, you can go on retreat if horribly injured or ill. We're all issued with a free Oyster card, a Met perk that unlocks London. I will more than get my moneyworth rinsing that.

There is some fearmongering. As police constables we are told that we are more under threat of terror attack than general members of the public. We should think of ourselves as walking targets, not tell unfamiliar people where we work, and cover our textbooks if revising in public. A spokesperson from the Directorate of Professional Standards (DPS) comes in to warn us how easy it is for people to get in trouble in this role. The Met receives a whopping 8-10,000 external complaints about police behaviour each year, and there are 20,000 internal disciplinary investigations. We are given some of the tamer examples of unprofessional behaviour; computer misuse (no surprise that police systems are not to be used as a criminal record search engine for friends, family, flatmates or anyone in our personal lives) to selling police kit on eBay.

Music starts blaring to introduce a PowerPoint montage of newspaper headlines about misconduct and crimes committed by former officers. Something about the pairing of these pretty shocking offences – such as accessing indecent images of children and sexually assaulting vulnerable victims – flashing up to the drumbeat of Coldplay's 'Yellow' reverberating around the hall really gets me. I turn to the girl with curls sitting next to me, who has looked my way at exactly the same moment. Eyes glinting, we dissolve into a fit of the giggles, sliding down into our chairs to avoid being seen. To this day my friends Mel, Lexi T and I fall about laughing if we hear this track. It doesn't really land that there might be some serious underlying issues around professionalism and integrity beyond minor infractions and the odd bad apple in the Met. I pay it no more thought as this information blurs with the next lecture and the day flows on.

In breaks, the Direct Entrants seek each other out, sharing stories of cluelessness and Bryn. Poor, poor Bryn, it turns out he is the only vetting point of contact for the entire Direct Entry programme, and everyone's vetting took far, far longer than six weeks. If I'd known, I'd have left the poor harassed man alone.

We are not the first Direct Entrants – there was an intake of thirty before us, and there will be another bunch along in a few months' time – but there's no mistaking how new the scheme is. Our basic training is the same as that of any new police constable: it starts with the thirteen-week basic Certificate in Knowledge of Policing, but we will have a further seven weeks of detective training bolted on. It will be intense – no leave or absence is allowed during the twenty weeks ahead – and we will be relentlessly assessed on what we learn. But where a police constable would have two years in uniform learning the ropes, we'll be straight into the job of detective constable in eight months' time.

We're split into two groups of fifteen and fourteen. Our sister group will stay here in Hendon, with the state-of-the-art facilities. We'll be heading to the other side of zone 5, Sidcup Training Centre, in deepest south-east London, practically Kent.

Sidcup, we discover when we turn up a couple of days later, is not the flashy police mecca of Hendon. Marlowe House is a grotty red-brick seventies tower block. At Sidcup it's not so much corridors of power as corridors of neglect. The building is run-down and peeling, full of broken furniture and useless rooms, and it is not long before my fellow classmates and I decide that we love it that way. It's crumbling but cosy and un-intimidating. When we head north for training days in Hendon we feel like country mice in the bright lights and big city.

For the first time since I left actual school, I am in a classroom with the same people all day, every day. I'm pleased to see that the girl with the curls is in my group. She's about the same age as me, striking, with a joyous smile that has to be well earned. She's warm and humorous and I think if anyone can take this in their stride she can.

It's taking a while for the others to come into focus. There are two girls who we nickname by their surnames, Fox and Lexi T, Joseph, still a mystery, Simon, slightly pompous, Sadie, a nice Kiwi who lives on a houseboat, Tom is young bouncy and posh, and Rick, an Aussie. Nath, who has a mop of black hair and looks like he's just out of the sixth form. Mia, who's so laid back she's hori-zontal. Georgia is pretty and petite, and already making eyes at Jake, who's smartly dressed and witty. Gabriel is a quiet authorita-tive presence in the corner. It turns out he used to work for British Transport Police, so maybe he's the only one of us not finding this overwhelmingly new and foreign.

Our class is split more or less 50:50 female to male, and we are all aged between about twenty-four and thirty-five. When it comes to voting in a Class Captain, whose most common task is to shout 'Class!', as the signal for everyone to leap to their feet when a member of staff enters the room, we vote in Rosie, a sens-ible head-girl type, who manages not to let the power go to her head. The other class has an ex-military guy with a touch of Alan Partridge in his late fifties who claims the position without a vote and takes to the job with dictatorial zeal.

We're all excited to be here, full of energy and optimism about what lies ahead. One early session, led by a no-nonsense northern instructor called Janey Mather, has a more confrontational vibe than we've encountered so far. As we sit in a semi-circle facing her, she points at us one by one and asks us what we used to do.

I'm interested to hear. We're a mixed bag: former lawyer, teacher, public servant, probation worker, sales, ex-military, stockbroker, hospital budget planner, advertising exec, journalist, project manager, IT consultant, researcher. Without fail she responds to every previous job with, 'That's all right, innit?' the implication being that we should have stayed where we were. Sometimes, even more forthrightly, she says 'Why did you give that up?' or 'That's a good job, why did you stop that to do this?'

No one knows how to answer. So far, having made it through, we'd been feeling like the chosen ones. We are all of us idealistic – hoping to play a part in something interesting, meaningful, helpful and real. Most of us took pay cuts to join the Met; there seems a mutual understanding that the fulfilment of doing something worthwhile will be the priceless remuneration. Now it seems she thinks we're stupid to be here.

She's certainly not cutting us any slack because of our 'detective-to-be' status. 'It's mad you're not doing time in uniform,' she says. 'You've not been drafted in to be pink and fluffy officers, you're still going to have to get your hands dirty.'

Which is her cue to show us a violent video of officers being attacked, having enormous knives pulled on them in custody, being mobbed, rolling around on the floor, being punched in the face, bricks flying, police horses rearing as they tackle riots.

'Right, that's all the niceties out of the way. Let's get going.'

*

Some of us had assumed that, as detectives, we wouldn't be conducting arrests. But to the dismay of a few, the curiosity of most and the delight of others, we learn at a very early stage that we absolutely will be, and now, at the ungodly hour of 7.30 a.m., we are filing into the gym for our first session of Officer Safety Training.

I've spent more time creating the right PE look than I have in anticipating the session itself. We were told to get a white T-shirt and write our surname in huge letters vertically down the front on the left breast in black marker. Looking around me, the interpretations of this instruction range from neatly marked to blurrily defaced. Makeshift uniforms aside, there's an uneasy tension in the air. I catch the eye of Lexi, who has THOMPSON trailing down her T-shirt. With her dark hair, pale face and expression of dread, she looks like Wednesday Addams. As we go through the preliminary bleep test – continuous running between two lines twenty metres apart in time to recorded beeps at an ever-decreasing time interval – her reluctance is comically palpable. I like her style. Although our induction included a presentation showing the heart rate of a firearms officer during a dawn raid (and though he was considerably fitter than most of us, it went through the roof), judging by this exercise the general police fitness bar is comfortably low. Even when the beeps get closer together, we are all able to do it without breaking a sweat.

Afterwards we are told to assemble 'parade style' in two rows, and taking our lead from those on the front row, we assume a typical army inspection pose, upright and at attention. The teacher, whose name badge reads Keith, a short, fat, furious middle-aged white man who tells us to address him as 'Staff', starts to weave his way round the front row, stopping in front of each person, standing that bit too close as he looks them up and down.

In the second row he spots that Mia's nails are a fair bit longer than the stubby maximum. 'Oops,' she says airily, 'must have forgotten to cut them.'

She has misread the situation. Staff visibly inflates with rage. 'FORGOT?! You FORGOT!' he bellows. 'Are you going to FORGET about your rape victim?'

Next he arrives at Mel. 'Did you FORGET to iron your T-shirt?' He prods a finger towards her.

'No, Staff, I don't iron any of my T-shirts,' she replies brightly.

Oh Lord, she's baited him.

'WHO ELSE IN HERE HASN'T HAD THE BASIC DECENCY TO IRON THEIR T-SHIRT BEFORE SETTING FOOT IN MY DOJO?' Keith insists on calling the smelly gym the 'dojo' in the manner of a sensei master.

A few of us put our hands up in solidarity. In reality of course, no one has ironed their T-shirt.

Spoiling for a fight now, he stomps past a few more pristine students until he's standing before me and notices my socks. Bingo! 'What are those?' he says very quietly through gritted teeth.

I go for pathetically apologetic. 'Sorry, Staff, I didn't have any white ankle socks, only trainer liners, which we were told not to wear so I thought these off-white ones would be better. Sorry.'

It doesn't wash. 'Grey socks!' he squawks. 'Why didn't you go and buy a pair this morning?'

'I left the house at 5 a.m. There weren't any shops open.'

'You could have gone yesterday afternoon, could you not?'

'Sorry.'

'Why didn't you?'

'I'm sorry.'

'Did you think you would get away with this FLAGRANT DISREGARD FOR UNIFORM?'

'Sorry.'

I'm trying not to engage in a battle I can't possibly win, yet he's still going on at me, getting more crimson by the second.

'WERE YOU AWARE THE POLICE IS A DISCIPLINED SERVICE? YOU MIGHT WANT TO THINK VERY LONG AND VERRRRRRRRRRRY HARD ABOUT YOUR CAREER CHOICE.' He stomps to the front of the class, screaming, 'PUT YOUR HANDS UP IF YOU ARE **EMBARRASSED** AT THE STATE YOUR COLLEAGUES HAVE SHOWN UP IN.'

A pause.

I look up from staring at the floor expecting to see all hands up, ready to resent them all. But everyone stands perfectly still, staring forwards in silent defiance.

'ALL OF YOUR HANDS SHOULD BE IN THE AIR!' he shrieks.

Not a flinch; institutionalised we are not. I want to laugh. It's such a powerful moment of solidarity as classmates reveal they're comrades. I really like these people. He turns on his heel and leaves the room defeated.

For the next few weeks we whistle the low birdsong coo and salute the rebellion sign from *The Hunger Games* whenever we venture within sight of the gym.

*

I've split up with Josh.

He's still in California as planned. I've left him for a friend of a friend who was paying me far more attention than my absent boyfriend. I can't believe how unaffected I feel about the break-up (although writing this now, it feels like my insides are being crushed and panic rises).

*

We now have structured days and a timetable of classes, although the curriculum is nothing like any syllabus I've ever studied. (See *Training to Become a Detective: The Syllabus* at the back of this book.) It's massive, and unfamiliar, with modules on everything from how to record and write in police style, to setting up a crimescene cordon and forensics, to suicide prevention, to domestic abuse, every session packed with information we have to stuff into our rusty brains. Practical scenarios and assessments begin, literally on day one. There will be internal theory exams every six weeks; the pass mark is 75 per cent and only one resit is allowed. On top of this there are fifty online courses to do in our own time and of course we have to get to grips with Blackstone's, the criminal law tome I bought so hopefully at the start of my long wait. We will need to know it back to front and upside down before sitting the notoriously tricky National Investigator's exam in the autumn.

Our main teacher during this time is Angus, a brilliant Glaswegian bear of a man for whom we all come to have the utmost respect. In his late sixties and retired as a Met officer, Angus has come out of retirement to teach. He really believes in the scheme, and wants to bring out the best in us. Over and over again, he tells us knowledge is power. 'If you don't know something, look it up, you're meant to be detectives after all!' Occasionally a session is taken by his sidekick, John, rattling through to get it over with, finishing with 'That all makes sense, yep?' but mostly it is Angus who leads us through the weeks of procedural information, piles and piles of it, role plays and criminal law. It's Angus who will make police officers of us.

For me this is a weird and wonderful time. I find every aspect fascinating, from the basic police officer's priorities on arrival at a crime scene (1. Preserve Life, 2. Preserve Scene, 3. Secure Evidence, 4. Identify Witnesses, 5. Identify Suspects). Much of it isn't intuitive and it's like learning a whole new language: Police Speak. Not just the famous Caution, 'You do not have to say anything, but it may harm your defence if you do not mention, when questioned, something which you later rely on in court. Anything you do say may be given in evidence', which we have to say when arresting someone, before interviewing someone and when they are finally charged (forgetting it, or mis-saying, renders all three procedures unlawful). There are mnemonics and acronyms designed to help, and every procedure has a mnemonic. Some of these have a notional relationship to what they describe. CUT, for example, which stands for C – Create distance, U – Utilise cover, T – Transmit, links to what you do when you see someone is armed with a knife. But I AM DADS CLINIC to remember suspect defences, CIAPOAR for dynamic risk assessment and decision-making, SAD CHALETS for major incident or TEDS PIE for interview question technique... they're so bizarre. We spend a fair bit of time wondering who on earth comes up with these things. Do they work on a team with the person who devises the police operation names or creates the e-fits (anyone remember the suspect who looked the spit of Zippy from *Rainbow*? – Google image it) as they too bring some rogue creativity to the job? As for the acronyms for police roles and departments, I am told about CAIT (Child Abuse Investigation Team) by the detective at court but mishear CAKE and believe it to be called that for the rest of the year. That said, the sex-offender management team is called JIGSAW, which I still find really odd. Then there are the extra little rules – you can't say 'dead' or 'murder' over the radio as this spreads panic if members of the public hear. Instead a no-longer-breathing victim might be described as 'life expired'. Some of us take to this better than others. Tom, whose voice is on the plummy side, is particularly keen on the lingo and appropriating police-type words with a newfound cockney twang: 'Tha's a bit Gucci, tha' (translation: 'that's fancy').

A police jargon glossary and rough syllabus of our course can be found at the back of this book. You are welcome.

*

'Preserve life' applies to others, and to ourselves. One of the first things we are taught is not to serve ourselves up. We are told not to go near the railway, fire or water. We are warned about the 'red mist' that descends at moments of high stress, when adrenalin clouds your assessment of danger. As for preserving the lives of others, our Emergency Lifesaving course makes me feel ashamed of how I have coasted through life without these essential skills. CPR should be on the school curriculum. Forget breathes, the kiss of life (I'm relieved; I've always felt stressed by the idea of saliva), it's the cardio that saves lives.

My schoolfriend, and new housemate, Gemma, gets the blow-by-blow lowdown of this lesson. For some time after, I become a living, breathing public-health announcement, wanting to tell everyone I know how to do chest compressions. (Push down over the centre of the breastbone to a third of the depth of the chest – use one hand on top of the other for an adult, just one hand for a child and fingers in a poking motion for a baby – and keep going.)

CPR can keep someone alive so they can be saved by defibrillation, which sky-rockets the survival rate to 90 per cent. Defibs are everywhere – in the back of all police response cars and on street corners – and you can call 999 to be told where the nearest is and access the code to use it. The defib will tell you what to do, but will not work on someone if they have flatlined. So doing the chest compressions keeps them going until paramedics and a defibrillator arrive.

In class we practise on tough plastic dummies without limbs, just torso and head, pressing down on the middle of the chest, pretty hard, to the beat of the song 'Stayin' Alive'. It's hard work – thirty compressions a minute whether it's an adult, child or baby – but easier if you hum the song and don't bother counting. When one of us tires, another takes over.

Every time we flag, Angus yells, 'You can swap, but never stop! DO NOT STOP.' You must carry on until the ambulance arrives.

*

Everything we learn is abstract. Imagine learning to drive without ever having got in a car, even as a passenger, or ever having seen a car for that matter. We take in the theory, and rehearse the look, feel and behaviour of being police constables – we play at turning the wheel – but it feels like make-believe.

Someone wise made the comment that passing a driving theory test doesn't make you a driver, and the same is true of this.

In role play after role play, we take it in turns to play suspects, victims and police investigators. The mild nature of the crimes – the theft of a bagel, an alleged arse-squeeze coupled with a phone theft; they always take place on Aerodrome Road for some reason – sitting oddly against the serious crime we learn about day in, day out.

Sometimes Angus plays the suspect and we see a version of him that throws us completely, as an unsuspected Glasgow hard man appears from under our teacher's gentle-giant exterior. You wouldn't have messed with him in his heyday. One role play grinds to a halt when a classmate, faced with Angus as an out-of-control suspect, shakily holds his police ID (warrant card) up to him. Angus responds, 'What does yer wee badge say there round yer neck? Officer CUNT?!'

When it comes to the assessments, there are two stooges who are wheeled out time and time again to play a tricky suspect. One of these, a pink-faced guy we nickname 'the Big Baby', is said to be a Direct Entry detective from a class a month ahead of us who has been frozen from progressing with the programme. The rumour is, he is being internally investigated. We discuss endlessly what he could have done. Allegedly, during his first trip to what would have been his first police station workplace, he went drinking with future colleagues after work. Later they all spilled out of the pub and he came back into the police station alone, where he saw fit to draw willies and swastikas on people's notepads and property. He then tried to minimise the fallout by admitting to drawing the childish and highly unprofessional ejaculating willies and hairy ball sacks but not to the swastikas. Now it was with the hand-writing and indentation expert, and the Big Baby is stuck in an eternal loop of playing the accused. If it's true it's outrageous he's still around. It's my first indication that among the many brilliant DCs in the Met, there are going to be some wrong 'uns.

Hendon's training centre has an entire building designated for role plays and practicals, complete with themed rooms. These include a fully kitted-out and realistic living room, kitchen and bed-room for role-playing crimes in domestic settings; a seedy nightclub with a chrome bar; even a post office. There is also a fake morgue with prosthetic dead people in body bags, some of them suitably battered with limbs missing, to replicate blunt-force trauma such as being hit by a train. There are also pretend dismembered body parts for DVI − Disaster Victim Identification − training, for ex-ample in the wake of a bomb going off, a plane crash or natural disaster. In our poor relation of a building, we play out scenes in empty corridors and a car park and half-furnished rooms. My fa-vourite, by far, is a retro seventies bedsit (but retro by abandon-ment for half a century rather than design), which we use for investigating the scene of the crime. It has a brown-and-orange floral print divan behind a padded screen, and a dining area and fridge stocked with random packets dated 'best before 1979'. The attention to detail extends to a photo of Donny Osmond in a frame, some old beer bottles, a red bra looped over a chair and an oil painting of a ship on a stormy sea above a perfectly arching splatter of fake blood across the back wall. Otherwise, the room is littered with weapons − fake guns, knives, even some nunchucks. Here, four of us at a time − the room won't fit more − attempt to establish vital evidence.

7

In the Police Training Bubble

We are all so different – different ages, backgrounds, life experiences; we share nothing in common, really – yet the fifteen of us bond over going through these experiences together. We are taught on an approximation of the police shift pattern of either early (7 a.m. to 3 p.m.) or late (2 p.m. to 10 p.m.), meaning it becomes hard to keep up with our outside worlds. Instead, our class turns into my support network as we learn the ropes to become fully fledged officers. Soon it's as if we checked out of our past lives at the door when we entered the Met.

Coffee and lunch breaks as well as after-work drinks on long summer evenings at the Iron Horse become vital times to decompress and a tonic for the intensity of the career we're gradually immersing ourselves in. Laughing at the absurdity of so many of the scenarios, and taking comfort in the fact that we're not alone in feeling out of our depth with certain aspects of the training, reaffirms essential confidence and self-belief. Being in it together is what makes these months a happy and exciting time.

Before long the fifteen of us have regressed to being teenagers – in jokes, cliques and silliness. My best friends are Mel and Lexi T. We're all newly single and around the same age. Mel, with her long blonde mermaid hair and golden-brown skin, is a hippy spirit who took off for her year abroad at uni and came back married and with a child. She's easy-going, enthusiastic and competent. She's left a responsible job as head of English in a London secondary school to work in the Met, and is the single parent of her eight-year-old daughter. Lexi T was a PR guru before the Met. She's super-sharp – in class she delivers answers so articulate it's as if they've been scripted – and has a droll, caustic wit. While I'm still licking my wounds after breaking up with Josh, Lexi T is going a bit wild after leaving a very serious and sensible decade-long relationship which ended after an awkward engagement. Mel and Lexi T are hilarious opposites. Where Mel is calm, Lexi T talks at a million miles an hour. Mel loves a hobby, from boxing to cheerleading, she is the sort who will mobilise a massive game of rounders in the park. Lexi T is small, has poker straight hair, hates sports, hates sun (wears Factor 100 sunblock), hates organised fun and every cold becomes bronchitis, if not fatal. They both think I am a joker and a bleeding heart. I love that the Met has room for all of us.

The three of us adopt Tom, the baby of the class, posh, impressionable and fresh from working in a think tank. Lexi takes it a step further and starts calling him her son. Meanwhile Georgia, who's a bit of a mean girl, Fox and good girl Rosie form a clique, though Fox, who is hilarious, forms a bridge between us. Soon Georgia starts going out with Jake and falls out with Lexi T... It is schooldays all over again.

*

'How many of you have seen a dead body?'

We are coming to the end of a dry lesson about packaging evidence. There are two raised hands but mostly people look uncomfortable and say nothing.

'You're going to see a lot of death; it's part of the job,' Angus tells us. 'We're now going to expose you to death in a controlled environment. If any of you want to leave the room at any point, then you can. Or, if you're bothered by what you see, you can come to us at the end.'

Apart from Nath, who is grinning ear to ear like an utter weirdo, the rest of us freeze and wait, wondering what's coming next. Are they going to wheel a corpse in? Angus returns with a shoebox covered in yellow health hazard tape.

'We're gonna ease you in gently; these are not too gory. You'll be seein' some more extreme ones later. The ones in this box are photographs from real sudden death scenes. I'll pass them round. Each booklet says what's happened on the front so if you dinnae want to look at what's inside, just pass it along.'

Angus opens the box, flicks through the first booklet, shakes his head, muttering 'Maybe a bit much,' puts it back and picks up another. The room is still and silent except for Nath, who's bobbing up and down in his chair with excitement.

Angus vets the next one, decides it's OK, and passes it to Fox. We all watch as she looks at the first page. No flinch. The second. Nothing. The third. We all see her eyes bulge, and then she looks long and hard at the final image, shudders and passes it on.

Soon there are about twenty of these booklets circulating. Photos of twenty people's mum, dad, grandma, grandad, son or daughter. Everyone but Nath is respectfully sombre and quiet. I feel intrusive looking at these photos as these images feel so deeply private to that person and their family. Most of them are taken in people's homes except for a few, which are in the woods. The first image is always what the officers will have seen when they set foot in this person's home uninvited – often a hallway or the kitchen, some immaculate, some a family mess of kids' toys, all of them normal, homely and in the circumstances painfully intimate. Only one is seedy, verging towards a crack den. The next photo is often a note on the table; the majority of the images are suicides.

Some of what we see are natural sudden deaths and the decomposition that follows when bodies are not found straight away. Wet or dry decomposition or blackening and bloating of dying and swelling with water in the bath. This transformation of the body in water is really shocking. A white person turns black. The inflation and engorgement are something to behold. One booklet which starts with a picture of two friendly well-fed dogs, ends with a corpse, more of a skeleton, devoid of flesh.

As the session goes on there's more blood, guts and gore from the box of horrors. There is even a self-decapitation where the head is clean off and sitting on a garage forecourt. People who've jumped from the top of a tower who are now a splatter on the pavement below, nothing intact, just a shoe, splat mark and globules of brain. Train suicides, river suicides where the body hasn't appeared for a week, hangings where the neck has split and bodily fluids run out like candle wax.

I can hear Nath across the room muttering 'Cooooool!' I am so furious at his total incomprehension that these are all real people who are no longer with us, not a TV scene, that I can't look at him.

All of them are deeply sad, but I find the hangings the most disturbing. This becomes something of a police phobia of mine. I desperately don't ever want to find someone hanging or see that in the flesh. Sometimes, after the photo of the note, you see a photo of legs dangling; sometimes they haven't been found for so long that the neck has stretched so they look more like giraffes. We're told that most people are not, as they think they will be, killed instantly by their attempt to kill themselves. The hints of those family members who will be left behind with unbearable grief are in every picture.

As we head home that afternoon we stand on the train platform numb, and no one talks.

*

'Alpha Kilo 13, Delta Uniform Hotel...'

Years ago, in a call-centre job as a car insurance claims handler during university holidays, I became a pro at using the phonetic alphabet. It actually used to really entertain me hearing what people come up with when they make up their own version. 'G for gnome' sticks in my mind. I volunteered to be the first to talk over the radio. So far we have tried using them from ten lines of cars away, and now I am to read the letters off the number plates. This should make me feel like DI Kate Fleming. Instead, as I read off the letters, my voice sounds high-pitched and childish over the airwaves and this makes me stammer. Then there is the fact that I can't make out what Angus is saying back to me. 'OK,' I say uneasily, 'Roger that.'

'Jess, don't say Roger that,' comes the crackly reply. 'That's not a thing. It's over.'

'Oops, OK. Over.' I feel ridiculous to be failing at something so basic.

*

We're on the second round of exams. Every day we try to stuff our heads with procedures, law, phrases and checklists. Some of the legislation is Olde English and has to be learnt by rote – like the Police and Criminal Evidence Act 1984, Section 117, which we may be summoned from a line-up to recite word perfect to an inspector: 'Where any provision of this Act (a) confers a power on a constable; and (b) does not provide that the power may only be exercised with the consent of some other person, other than a police officer, the officer may use reasonable force, if necessary, in the exercise of the power.' Translation: 'you can use reasonable force when necessary'. Mel saves the day by turning it into a beatbox rap to the tune of 'Fresh Prince of Bel-Air'.

I love an exam, I've always preferred them to writing long essays. The irony of that is not lost on me as I tap away now, sharing my story with you. A couple of the class have to do resits, which knocks their confidence a bit. Shorty is a whizz at exams and tests and makes no secret of it. While we are all checking and double-checking against the clock he makes a show of finding the exams easy, putting his pencil down, yawning loudly and leaving the room early as if to make a point. Not all of us are team players.

*

We're in the classroom looking at a table laden with guns and bullets of all shapes and sizes. We've been given a talk by a self-confessed 'gun nut' from a Met firearms unit and now we're encouraged to pick up, handle and examine them (they're all disabled). For the first and very much the last time I pick up a Glock. I'm surprised by how heavy it is.

Tom learns that pointing a gun at me gets a good reaction – like a cat when you put a cucumber on the floor near it (YouTube it). He points it at my face and I immediately drop to the floor. My takeaways from this lesson are: one, a rifle bullet can travel three miles. It will go through people and not stop. A bullet fired down at the floor will carry on and on and on along the ground. And two, I hate guns.

*

As spring turns into summer, the weather is surprisingly good and everything's blooming, except my new romance. I jolt awake in bed next to him one morning and all the feelings for Josh I'd suppressed are coursing through me and very real. It wakes me up to the fact that this was a rebound, of course it was, and dead in the water in light of the fact that I'm still totally in love with someone else. Flooded with regret I reach out to Josh asking to meet. He grants me that. I apologise and beg for another chance but he kindly tells me no. It's too late, he's seeing someone else. I am so heartbroken, but the agony that I've brought all this on myself and can't undo what's done is the worst bit. How I'll ever make peace with that I don't know. Luckily I'm largely distracted by training.

*

We do a lot of our role plays, practical lessons and assessments outside. Hendon has a designated forecourt for this sort of thing. On the flipside, we have the staff car park.

It is in the car park that we learn about how to establish a police cordon (the taped-off area round a crime scene) – where to put the inner cordon (to protect evidence) and where to put the outer cordon (to keep the public from invading or trampling around the scene: here the guiding principle is that you can always make the cordon smaller, so go big). It is a very windy day and tape is blowing all over the place as we tie it to wing mirrors and saplings in the car park. We think we've nailed it, but our instructor tells Lexi T that we've all walked over the 'dead body' and now we are standing on it. We have also excluded it from the crime scene cordon. An X of yellow and black caution tape, outside our cordon entirely, marks the spot.

On another day, we are in the car park to practise stopping and searching each other for drugs and weapons. There are four types of search: Initial, Detailed, Strip (which has to be carried out in a custody suite; the suspect is stripped naked, half their body at one time) and Intimate, that is, orifices (which has to be done by a doctor). We're dealing with the first two, which can be done in a public place. The search can be done free-standing (like an airport search, arms out), prone (lying on the floor) or wall (facing the wall, feet far apart, leaning hands on the wall so the detainee can't run or suddenly move).

First things first, blue gloves on. Double glove for better protection from needle pricks. (Police School is full of little details that hint at hidden risk.) We have the power to detain a person (force them to stop and stay), then to demand they take off the following but nothing else. The mnemonic is:

J – Jacket
O – Outer garment
G – Gloves

We're told to frisk – that is, pat, from head to feet using hands and fingertips, splitting the body into quarters (eight segments front and back). Honestly, imagine being paired up with any one of your colleagues, male or female at random, and then being told to thoroughly run your hands over their entire body. It's so uncomfortable.

At first one of Keith's team-mates tells us to use the back of our hand in certain areas such as tracing over the bra, as if it's not pervy if the palm isn't involved. Later he slightly shamefacedly announces it'll be same-sex searching only from here on in and apologises regarding the incorrect info on the back of the hand boob check, 'So please stop doing that immediately.'

On the first run no one touches anyone. We just pretend. Angus tells us to get a grip (but not literally).

Next, we attempt a wall search. I'm paired with Georgia, Lexi T's sworn enemy, a little pocket rocket with no meat on her bones. She's leaning forward in a saggy hoody. I stop when I find a little bag of white powder tucked into her trousers. After the practice is over and the instructor asks if everything was found, Georgia gleefully shakes her head and produces a knuckleduster that I've missed from the front pouch in her hoody. She does a little dance and holds it over her head, pretending it's as heavy as an anvil. 'Oh my God, I can't believe you didn't find this! It's HUGE!' she crows.

On the third attempt things get competitive. Half the class are given something to hide on their person (flick knives, fake drugs, and so on) and the partner has to find it. To make sure the goods are never found, girls jam them in their bra and boys down their trousers. No one finds a thing!

'C'mon people, you're gonna be assessed on this,' balls Angus across the car park. 'If ye don't do it properly you will all FAIL.'

As there's an odd number of boys, Tom gets paired with Angus. This time he's really trying, patting away industriously. As he gets to the trousers there's a sudden cough and a splutter and he realises his fingers are wedged into the waistband front and centre of Angus's boxers.

*

When I carelessly threw my life with Josh away, I moved in with Gemma in Bethnal Green near where he used to live. She must think I am the phantom flatmate. I'm either up hours before she wakes, or I'm back at midnight, emerging from my bed after she's left for work. Catching up with friends outside work has tailed off too. Weeknight dinners and after-work drinks are impossible to manage with the late finishes and early starts of the shift pattern. I used to be so sociable; now my friends think I'm ignoring them.

At first I don't really notice the drop in the quantity of catch-ups with friends because any loss on that front is compensated by the intensity of our weekend meet-ups. Friends and acquaintances can't get enough of my Met stories, thrilled to live vicariously through me. I'm more than happy to oblige, regaling them with the most extreme, bizarre tales, paying forward war stories I've been told. At parties it seems that becoming a detective has made me a magnet. I bask in the spotlight, enlightening them about the existence of semen sniffer dogs, and taser training, which involves a guy in a suitably padded bodysuit running and screaming at trainees with the biggest machete imaginable. I feel lucky to be on the cusp of experiencing a job so interesting it provokes this sort of reaction from my friends. Also, I'm a little relieved we're not discussing my love life any more.

*

A lifetime ago, during the early stages of the recruitment process, we were asked to pick our top six of the thirty-two boroughs within greater London and the Met to help allocate the police station where we will be based for the rest of our two-year probationary period. All I knew at that stage was that I wanted to be exposed to real crime on a busy borough, be in the centre of it all and have a breezy commute. So, naively believing that what is reported in the news is a direct representation of all the most serious crime in the capital, I googled 'where is there most crime in London?' Westminster came out on top, so that's what went at the top of my list. Turns out that's what we all put down. As for the other choices, when faced with so much unknown, I put down central boroughs I was familiar with, that would be easy to get to – Tower Hamlets, Southwark, Islington. Now, about three months in, we receive notification of our borough postings. I am delighted to be posted to Tower Hamlets (which during our training hooks up with Hackney to become Central East). It's local! I can't wait to just walk round the block to get to work.

*

We have been handcuffing each other for weeks. The rigid handcuffs that we use in the UK are put on by smashing the closed ring on to the wrist just in front of the wrist bone, then pushing the second wrist in. For weeks the red, green, blue, purple rainbow bruise rings around tender wrists we all sport are a reminder that this takes some practice.

I'm pleasantly surprised to learn that handcuffing doesn't automatically form part of an arrest. I'm reassured that as detectives we will hold a relatively low conflict frontline role, and that using handcuffs in an arrest isn't a given: they constitute a use of force and have to be justified. Except, I could probably justify using them in most cases as I'm small, and you'd have to be particularly puny not to be able to overpower me.

There's no two ways about it, these 'bracelets' are uncomfortable. They're heavy, they dig into skin, they knock bone. They have an edge that leaves red marks. And that's when you know what you are doing. For our assessment of this skill we are paired up to handcuff each other three ways – in a simple front stack, to the back and when resisting arrest, having been pulled to the floor onto a blue gym mat. Tom and I are paired up. I show him my party trick that I can wriggle out of a handcuff on all but the tightest clamp setting while we wait for our turn to perform.

We take it in turns cuffing each other, get the nod that we've both passed and head for a break. As I turn to him in delight that we've done it, Tom presents me with his bleeding wrist, a trickle of blood running the length of his forearm where I sliced him with the cuff. He'll never let me live this one down.

*

We're doing interview training – but on each other. For these role plays, which are recorded in the high-tech interview rooms at Hendon, we're split into three groups. Three people in the interview, playing the part of the interviewing officer, the suspect and the solicitor, while the remaining two listen and watch the chaos unravel from the monitoring station outside.

This time we're practising holding it together in testing situations. Each time something is thrown into the mix to derail the interview into going farcically wrong and the interviewer has to stoically keep calm and in control, trying to heave it back on track and carry on. The result is a week of laughing so hard my face and stomach muscles ache.

One interview starts with low-level irritation. Our supervisor, John, tells the person playing the solicitor to start tapping their pen on the table during the interview. It's dealt with politely, the obstacle overcome, interview completed. Too easy.

In another I'm playing the suspect in a stabbing and am asked to draw the weapon I've described someone else as having. Diligently I take the biro and draw a chef's knife to scale. At the end of the debrief session one of our supervisors asks me to sign my doodle so he can put it up on the staff noticeboard. Cue howls of laughter; some of my classmates are almost crying. I don't get it. Apparently on their monitor it looked like I'd drawn a dildo. I scrunch up the picture and bin it.

As the day progresses we rise to the acting challenge, taking our disruptive roles to the extreme. I've never seen John so mischievous. He is delighting in ramping up the distraction briefs as the day progresses.

The next interview sees collusion between the solicitor and the interviewee. The solicitor blocks questions and blatantly coaches the suspect. They even exchange a high-five at one point.

In another, we stand on the sidelines and watch and listen in as the suspect played by Lexi T flirts outrageously with the interviewing officer. She's really hamming it up. 'Sorry, Officer,' she coos. 'What was the question again? I got lost in your eyes.' She bats off another question with a dreamy 'Have you been sent to seduce me into a confession?' To another she purrs, 'I'll answer yours if you answer mine.'

For my turn playing the suspect I'm told to be really aggressive and to physically get in my interviewer's personal space. Jake doesn't see it coming. I start being bolshie and exasperated with my 'no comment' before getting angrier and angrier, beating my fists on the desk, yelling 'NO FUCKING COMMENT.' He's actually really thrown but it's too late to back down. I'm in character, blinkered and spurred on, hearing my audience laughing outside. I start shunting my chair closer to him round the table so that I am bearing down on him, to which he responds by retreating until I'm chasing him round the desk like a wild thing.

I take it a bit far but am not even in the same league as one of the instructors of another group. He put his hands in his trousers and pretended to start wanking in a role play and then, in the debrief, chastised the interviewer as she refused to go on with proceedings rather than defusing the situation. What the defusing technique would be in this situation, we're not quite sure.

*

Sometimes it feels like the Met has eclipsed more than my weekday evenings. At the end of August, I escape from London for my first time away since joining the Met. My aunt is throwing a weekend festival. She and my uncle are vets who live up a mountain with views to die for, my four cousins, a small flock of sheep, four dogs, two cats and a hare that lives in the hallway. I adore being up there with them. The location itself is unspoilt and stunning and that's before my aunt worked her magic and created a dreamscape. It's a feast for the eyes; a giant tipi tent stands before the rolling hills beside a meadow of daisies and the campsite. Inside, beneath ribbons of bunting and wildflowers, there are straw-bale sofas and an amazing bar. At dusk everywhere is lit up with a thousand fairy lights and firepits. I'm so ready for this sheer escapism from the dull ache of losing Josh and to relax and enjoy the music, performances, drinking, dancing, dining, win rounders, night hiking. I have a huge extended family and a whole heap of cousins, over thirty at last count, and I can't wait to catch up with everyone. On arrival I realise just how knackered I am and how much I need the break, but all anyone wants to talk about is the Met. I want to chill, and recharge, and just be my old self; I don't want to tell the stories or be in that extreme world all the time. But even in this rural idyll, working in the Met feels like a high-vis vest. It's neon and I'm wearing it.

*

Having been to visit our police stations and boroughs for the first time, we come into class a couple of days later to unexpected news.

'Sadie has decided to leave the scheme,' announces Angus.

'What?!' we all say. We're stunned. Sadie was a probation officer in her previous life, and already has a working knowledge of the criminal justice system. She's bright, friendly, considerate and has flown through Police School so far. She looked like she would go far in the Met.

'Did she say why?' we ask.

Nothing. Apparently she has spent a day in the police station, decided it's not for her and gone back to her old job. I feel disappointed for her. She's come this far, I wish she'd given it more of a chance.

'Ah well,' sighs Angus. 'The Met's not for everyone.'

*

And then, just like that, school's out. It's been twenty weeks – five non-stop intense months; we've slogged through three rounds of exams and endless assessments. It's a beautiful summer's day and it feels like this should be a time to relax and coast to the end of the course before the real work starts on borough the very next week.

Instead, our final lesson at Police School, one I've been curious about since I first saw it on the course planner, is 'Sudden Death: The Message'. It's a lesson about how to break the news to someone that their loved one is dead. None of us can believe that a session on breaking the worst news someone will ever hear was planned to be the last lesson together before we graduate.

Even Angus visibly winces as he introduces the session. 'Now before we start, we have raised the suitability of teaching this lesson at this point with the course schedulers. The outcome is

TBC so we'll just have to soldier on and hope that future classes will have a lighter class to end on.'

First we're told to ask relatives to sit down to stop them from collapsing. People react to bad news in different ways; some collapse, some attack (and it's more difficult for them to attack and injure you from a seated position). We're not told what to say when you break the news that will ruin someone's life. In that situation there's common sense and apparently a helpline you can ring.

Instead, we have a PowerPoint on what not to say. This includes, but isn't limited to:

'At least you have other children.'

'It was God's will.'

'I know exactly how you're feeling.'

If no one answers the door, we are told not to put a note through the door to deliver the message.

'Are these for real?! Have people actually made these mistakes?' Mel asks incredulously as we pass round the takeaway sheets of 'Don'ts'. It's a small red flag that sometimes empathy is not ubiquitous in the Met.

'Sadly, I believe so,' Angus replies, shaking his head.

*

We end the day unable to believe that this is it — the next time we see each other will be at graduation day. Four of my class will be coming with me to Tower Hamlets: Rick, Gabriel, Shorty and Mia, along with John and Kevin from our sister class. Mel, Lexi T and Tom are going to Croydon. Police School has been our bubble — hard work, yet also insulated and oddly remote from the real thing. Now the real work starts. I just hope I never have to call that helpline.

8

Detectives in Development
Autumn 2018

Our first official day in the police station. I have made it here by hot-footing it to the train, stomping to the Tube, changing Tube, and the cherry on top is a bus. My first thought on crossing the police-station threshold, going from reception through the heavy security door to the realm the public never enter, is 'This place reeks of weed.' As it turns out, the combination of the furnace-like temperature of our police station with the bulging haul in the Seized Property room kicked out that sweet aroma most days. It becomes the comforting smell of this, my second home.

I'm not, as I hoped, living a few streets away and rolling out of bed to walk to work. Two weeks ago, Gemma's boyfriend became her fiancé and moved in. And now, with no warning whatsoever, I have to move out – with nowhere else to go. My cousin Rachael has, not for the first time, come to my rescue in a big way. So, this weekend, I packed up my worldly goods and headed across London to stay with her, her husband Paddy and their newborn baby Evie. Feeling too poor to pay for a taxi, I heaved my bags an hour and a half diagonally across London (east to south-west, from zone 2 to zone 6, by Tube and train). The fact that I can physically carry everything I own across London is some kind of achievement, but not one that feels good. It's been almost ten years since I was a backpacker – how have I hit thirty without owning so much as one piece of furniture? I thought I'd be married with kids by now; instead I'm being scooped up by my cousin and her husband in their family wagon. The straps of one of those heavy-duty Ikea bags I've used leave red indents on my shoulders that stay for days.

But I love being with Rachel, Paddy and Evie in their family home. They have made me so welcome, and from the moment I turn my key in the lock and step inside, I feel warm and relaxed staying with them. And baby Evie, the Little Bear as I call her, is pure joy. I've never been bothered by babies before, I'm usually all about the puppies, but she changes everything. It's just a shame that my commute is, once again, an absolute bitch at two hours door to door.

*

The police station is – I think it now and every day thereafter – a glorious shambles. To think I once worked in slick high-rise offices with too much glass, views of the Shard, breakfast provided in an open-plan shiny kitchen with soft-close laminate cabinets. Here the floor creaks beneath ancient lino. Plastic bags full of discarded uniform clutter the stairwells and gather at the dead ends of corridors. We are led on a walking tour of the building by DC Birdy Harris, our mentor for our development period, which will be spent getting up to speed practicing on real people before we sit our big National Investigators Exam in a couple of months and are fully fledged.

As we make our maiden voyage, we see there are more than a few junk rooms. 'Oooh, nothing to see in here,' says Birdy, opening a door to reveal a messy mountain of exhibits (evidence from cases), case files and box upon box of interview discs, and then slamming the door quickly shut, before the smell of dead rat can waft into the corridor. Another room is a chair graveyard, packed full of abandoned ones stacked from floor to ceiling. There are specialist units that have blinds pulled down over the internal windows as their work is not for general viewing. East End born and bred, as Cockney as they come, Birdy knows everyone and everything. After thirty years on the front line as a Detective

Constable – he never went for climbing the ranks – he now has the task of steering us through our development period. It will be three months of preparing for the National Investigators' Exam (NIE) and consolidating our training in real situations, before we are thrown into the tiger pit of the main office, where we will be doing the job properly. Dressed with immaculate, military precision – you never see him without a blazer, cravat and shoes you could see your face in (sometimes he adds a Trilby hat) – he is chatty and jokey in an old-school way, and instantly puts us at ease. Birdy, we soon realise, is a Tower Hamlets legend.

In the main investigations office, where we will soon be working, the desktop computers were new at the turn of the millennium. We're shown a staff room for our floor which comprises a sink and then a carpeted area with five mismatched, different height tables but not a single chair. 'No one really uses this room,' says Birdy. An alcove with an aluminium water fountain has been criss-crossed in police cordon tape, like a spider-webbed doorway at Halloween, and labelled with a hastily scribbled 'DO NOT USE. Fault reported'. (In Mel's police station they found Legionella bacteria in the water supply so all the water fountains were off limits.) I'll learn soon enough that something is always broken here. The building smacks of policing budget cuts but there is, nonetheless, something comforting about it, perhaps a nod to our beloved former Sidcup home. I would far sooner this than a sterile atmosphere and it would be disheartening to think that the Met's pressured budget was being poured into police station 'frills' rather than frontline salaries.

Birdy's own office shows evidence of his passion for the Royal family, especially the Queen. 'I see you love Liz,' I venture, as my eyes dart from the HRH calendar, to a coronation mug, to the Queen in all her finery on his mouse mat.

Birdy shoots me a filthy look, and responds, deadpan, 'I presume you speak of Elizabeth the Second, by the Grace of God, of the United Kingdom of Great Britain and Northern Ireland and of Her other Realms and Territories, Queen, Head of the Commonwealth, Defender of the Faith?'

'That I do,' I deadpan back.

He bursts out laughing, as does everyone. 'You're a good kid.'

The morning ends in a tatty classroom with blue plastic lecture seats with desk attachments, all left-handed. The lights are dimmed and we're shown a projected slideshow, 'Day in the life of a DC'.

'Your day,' starts Birdy, narrating over the images, 'will start with the question "Got anyone in the bin?"' (any prisoners?)

It will be a while until the reality he goes on to describe truly dawns on us.

*

For the duration of our development period, we have our own little backwater office. Here we are incubated and shielded, away from the chaotic open floor that is the main investigations office. It's a safe space for us to experience our first taste of work life on borough. On the whiteboard Birdy has drawn a big chart with a list of key skills and a checkbox for each of our names:

	Custody familiarisation	Arrest	Stop and search	Suspect interview	Conflict resolution	Victim care	Witness statement	Response
Rick								
Simon								
Jess								
Mia								
John								
Gabriel								

The aim is that we familiarise ourselves with these skill areas, and become proficient in them before we join our teams as detectives. We'll need two ticks next to each skill. No more practising on the Big Baby and each other, no more goofing about in the car park. Now we will be conducting the tasks we've trained for on real people, and in real situations.

I now see that completing training was a false summit. Stepping into a police station and entering this new world it's as if I've rounded the corner and a whole new peak has revealed itself, so high that it was previously obscured by the clouds. But Birdy, robust, experienced, old-school, fond of an inappropriate joke but never inappropriate himself, has our backs. He believes in us and that makes all the difference.

*

There is about to be a big fat tick in the box for Custody Familiarisation as we're going down to the basement en masse to take a look at the custody suite of twenty cells.

Never having been arrested, I have not set foot in a police cell before. From this day onwards there won't be a day when I'm not down here; it's where we interview.

Through the rabbit warren of corridors in the police station we trail down to the custody suite, greeted by the stench of weed as we round the corner past the property store. While every police station has a different custody layout, they are variations on a theme – always down in the bowels of the building, always devoid of natural light. Our senses heighten as Birdy punches in the code for the first airlock door and it gives the satisfying click of an old-fashioned safe. We all cram into the cupboard-sized vestibule, then hear the click of the second door before entering an unforgettable new realm.

What I see is not unlike a dystopian hotel. In front of me there is a hexagonal raised platform – the check-in desk – with six check in/out slots, each shielded from the other by a partial wall and manned by custody sergeants. Towering over everyone on their plinth, custody sergeants are usually officers who have already put in a long stint at the Met and might be seeing out the final stretch to retirement working twelve-hour seated shifts. 'Met gut' often comes with the territory. They authorise or deny every arrest and take full responsibility for that person for the twenty-four hours they may be in custody. Twenty-four hours is the time limit in custody before a charge, although it can be extended to thirty-six hours in exceptional circumstances. If you're arrested on suspicion of terrorism it might be twenty-eight days. It blows my mind that when Tony Blair was Prime Minister he tried to pass a bill that would allow police to hold terror suspects for ninety days without charge.

We're instructed not to touch or lean against the wall as there is a panic strip at hip height that snakes around every surface in case of attack. Seconds after Birdy utters this warning, one accident-prone member of our gaggle pushes a door too vigorously, smashing it into the strip. The alarm siren squeals out and six officers leap into action and come stampeding towards us to help, adrenalin pumping. They look pissed off to find it's just one of us probationers.

There is also a team of DDOs (Dedicated Detention Officers) who wear blue and look after the needs of everyone detained in here, taking fingerprints, etc. If we're sticking with the hotel theme, they would be butlers providing the room service, food and beverages – but not a service that indulges the whims of the guests. Talking of food, we pass the boxes and boxes of ambient (I don't understand what the food consists of, to not need refrigeration) microwaveable meals piled up, ready to be handed out with bendy cardboard spork. If the privilege of a limp plastic knife is extended, a big 'K' is marked on the meal carton to ensure that it gets collected in after the delicious dinner has been devoured so there is no risk of shanking (stabbing with a crude, usually homemade, weapon).

En route to the cells we nip into the drying room. 'All quite self-explanatory,' says Birdy. This is where wet exhibits (something taken from a crime scene that can be used as evidence), usually items of clothing, are dried. They might be soggy due to rainwater, a spin cycle, urine, semen or, judging from the metallic stench of dried blood in this place, a catastrophic bleed. Today there is the sad sight of one small child's blazer hanging in there from a fatal post-school stabbing.

In the medical room next door a doctor is on hand 24/7. Aside from the usual health conditions, people come into custody in varying states, from blind drunk, to drugged or black and blue. They could have quite severe injuries that haven't been apparent on arrest, for instance their hand might have slipped onto the blade while stabbing someone in a bloodied frenzy. They may also need intimate samples taken, a few sprigs of pubic hair, a genital swab or a little bit of blood.

Next door to that is the room where forensics and biometrics are taken – fingerprints and strip searches. Back in the day, people would be asked to squat to ensure they weren't carrying anything inside them but now a same-sex officer will peer into the orifice to check there isn't anything up there that shouldn't be. This isn't standard procedure for everyone. If someone has a criminal record and hides things up their bottom (aka prison pocket) they will flag up on the PNC (Police National Computer) as 'Concealer'.

'No one ever said being in custody was glamorous,' says Birdy.

Then we reach the interview rooms: this will be our zone. Every arrest and stay in custody leads here. These would be not so much the lounge of the dystopian hotel as the laundry cupboard – cramped, windowless little cubby holes with carpeted walls to soundproof them so interviews can be recorded clearly. In a way, these are the cosiest-looking places in custody, but not for the suspect. For them they are probably yet another stressful space where they give their side of the story. Also, they are usually swelteringly hot and have no air flow. Panic and the fact that people don't tend to shower during the twenty-four hours they're in custody – there is only one monitored communal shower cubicle – means an interview is often none too fragrant.

Finally, the twenty cells, with the majority on a male corridor and a few on a short female corridor. The UK prison population is 95 per cent male; unsurprisingly the gender split of our guests here mirrors that hefty majority. Someone is booting off in one of the cells, body-slamming the door, slapping the walls with the standard issue blue PE mat mattress. Judging by the bored expression of the DDO standing near the door, the muffled shouts coming from within have been going on for a while.

Birdy collects a key from the main desk and we head off to look inside an empty cell. It's empty for a reason – a whiteboard in reception reads 'M4 closed for maintenance – ligature points'. We're told that there's a risk someone with a death wish could hang themselves from the nicks and grooves in the breeze-block walls of this cell where the grouting has eroded away. It's hard to see how, considering that hairbands, hoodie toggles, belts, shoelaces and any conceivable 'noose' is confiscated on arrival. If someone's clothing poses a risk of harm or is taken for evidence, then the guests are given a grey tracksuit with matching lace-less slip-on plimsolls. Birdy says people have used the plastic seal strips from evidence bags to garotte themselves before now, 'so make sure you bin them'. It's hard to fathom that these seemingly extreme measures are in place because all these worst-case scenarios have actually happened in the past. Last year there were 52,726 self-harm incidents in prison custody. It's not uncommon for a prisoner to be placed on constant watch where the risk of self-harm and suicide is deemed to be high. The cell door will be kept ajar and a gaoler or probation officer will sit facing into the cell with eyes on the prisoner for the entire time they are there.

Before we enter the empty cell, we examine the door and are shown a spy hole and the wicket, a pull-down reinforced-glass screen that can be slid down to reveal a rectangular letterbox to deliver a meal and talk through. You can even conduct an interview through this hole if someone refuses to leave their cell or is not to be trusted in a small room. The door is opened with a large brass key. No contactless warrant cards and pins for us, we're old-school here. The door is the heaviest I've ever encountered, with the exception of the time I went on a tour of a naval submarine. 'Do NOT get your hand in the way of this one,' says Birdy. 'It will chop your fingers clean off. I'll show you a picture of what that looks like later.' I can believe it. In we go.

The second I step in I want to be out.

The cell itself reminds me of a swimming-baths shower cubicle... without the shower. There's certainly no means of washing in here, not even a basin. It's about two by three metres and bare of everything but a bench (the 'bed') moulded out from the wall. On the bench is a re-purposed thin blue PE mat, the only 'soft' surface in here, which suffices as a kind of mattress. There is no pillow or blanket, as these can be tools for suicide or destruction, for example ramming them down the metal toilet bowl in the corner and flooding the cell. Toilet paper is also held back. If you're behaving, these luxuries will be granted; though not the pillow, there are never pillows. Black writing spray-painted on the rough plaster ceiling boldly states: 'You are being filmed. Cameras operate in these cells.' Everything in this room smacks of hopelessness.

Now the suicide risk makes more tangible sense to me. The idea of being locked up here for twenty-four hours is horrific, and for some this might be the start of being incarcerated for a very long time. Imagining the stress of it leaves me with a sympathy for the incarcerated that I never lose.

We can just leave, and we do, the colossal door banging shut behind us.

'Right,' says Birdy. 'Any questions? Let's go round the back and you can ask me over breakfast.'

*

Any spare moment we can, Birdy takes us 'round the back' to the local greasy spoon for breakfast (lunch isn't really a thing in the Met) or the pub, depending on the hour. Birdy's an open book, and at the end of the day likes nothing better than to light up a cigar, sip on a Neck Oil beer and tell us his life story. Soon we know all about his kids, his grandkids, the ex-wife, his new wife – he whips out his phone to show us pictures – what the first dance was at this second wedding, how he knew the Kray brothers, that his mum has an African Grey pet parrot, how much he loves West Ham. As soon as he sits down he's off, heading down this tangent and that, and no one gets much of a word in edgeways. He's a wonderful character. With me he's fatherly – he always says I remind him of one of his daughters. One day, when I mention that I want to work in the Murder Squad, he says 'I can fix that for you, darlin',' and quick as a flash he's taken a picture of me and texted it to an ex-colleague with the message: 'This young detective wants to work on the murder team can you sort it out?' I laugh it off, because I can't believe this is how someone would get a run at such a popular unit, and although not by the book, the good heart in his intentions is obvious.

We soon realise how lucky we are to have Birdy. In Croydon and Bromley, Mel, Lexi T, Tom, Rosie and Georgia have a sergeant for their mentor, a woman so tough and unrelenting she has made a few of them cry at work, which is some feat. Her standards are impossibly high and Tom in particular is a target – she constantly questions his competence, micro-monitoring his every move and finding it wanting. When it comes to holiday (we have been going for five months already without a break), she insists that they all take leave on the same week or not at all – something impossible for Mel, who for childcare needs to work around school holidays. The Met might have opened its doors to us as Direct Entrants, but this woman makes life within it unbearable for them. Tom considers quitting. He says he's going to but every time we see him he still hasn't; he ploughs on.

*

Although there's nothing about this station that Birdy doesn't know, he's as new to this scheme as we are, and our development period has an ad hoc feel to it, like he's making it up as we go along. He's cheerfully rough and ready, and perhaps not as concerned with Met protocol and systems as he should be. He takes it lightly, punctuating even the hairy moments with 'It's all a bit of a laugh, innit?'

Today Hannah, Birdy's sidekick, tells us to grab our PPE bags (stab vest and belt with cuffs and weapons), get kitted up and meet her in the yard by the minibuses. 'We need to get you some arrests, so let's go and nick some slags.'

'Slags' is a Met-wide slang that is used by many frontline officers across all boroughs across London, a derogatory term for someone, male or female, who is in and out of custody. Not to be confused with the other derogatory term for a 'promiscuous woman' I'm still getting used to the way everyone talks. It's not just that everything is fucking this and fucking that, it's also a lack of filter. Hannah, who's Mancunian – an accent not much heard in these parts (my own northern vowels stand out a mile) – has her heart in the right place, but I wouldn't describe her as by the book.

We're sent off to get our gear on. My PPE (Personal Protective Equipment) is still wrapped in the plastic it came in, box-fresh and untried. I go into the ladies' toilet on our floor to change. Staring at the metal scourer on one of the basin rims I wonder what would possess someone to wash dishes in a toilet sink, before promptly starting to use the place as a changing room. I unpack and assemble my tool belt on the damp loo floor, placing all the weapons in their individual holsters before strapping them on. When I finally clip it on it's so big that I have to clutch it to stop it falling off. Lastly I velcro on my Met vest, which is quite heavy because of the dense breastplate, designed to stop a knife point from entering the torso. I emerge with the vest on too tight but it feels weirdly good, like a perma bear-hug. I keep thinking about a story I was told at my vest fitting months ago about how a member of public went to give a policer officer a high five. In reciprocating the officer's vest rose up, at which point the person plunged a knife into their exposed stomach (the officer survived).

We wander down to the gated yard, all the gear, no idea. Past custody, where as usual someone is banging something in a cell very loudly. Hopefully mattress on the floor rather than head on the door.

Hannah, already in the driving seat of what we come to call the 'the fun bus', tells the seven of us to climb into the back of the van. When you sit down in a Met vest, I now learn, the thing rides up so that the structured shoulder pads end up level with your ears, giving the impression of a shy turtle.

This is our first time; we are all as clueless as each other.

The plan for today is to drive around the borough going from address to address to track down wanted people, arrest them in their homes and then haul them back to custody. Wanted for what, you might ask? Well, wanted for anything, Hannah's not fussed. 'Crime's crime, innit?'

It's a shock to me. I had never realised that as well as those already in custody, there are always, never-endingly, hundreds of serious known criminals in the borough awaiting arrest – and they are all on this list.

Hannah passes us back a laptop and says to just look on the wanted system and pick someone to go for.

'What, pick anyone?' I ask. We look at the system. Each entry is a small form with basic information: name of victim, the offence they're wanted for, some of the details, the day and date of the incident, the grounds for the arrest and, if they're a repeat customer, a mug shot.

Today, proximity is the priority. We filter the system like searching for a flat to rent on Right Move.

'Remember to check what they flash,' says Hannah, as she bumps a car and scrapes the wall manoeuvring the van out of the awkward spot in the cramped police yard where it's been parked by the previous user. She means the section titled Officer Safety Warning where a suspect can be marked with a red flag warning, such as Violent, Weapons, Contagious.

I've always thought of myself as pretty comfortable with risk, but Hannah's gung-ho approach is sitting even more uncomfortably than my vest. I know that making arrests is something we have to know how to do – every police officer has the power of arrest for their whole career – but I had envisaged the arrest coming at the end of working on a case, maybe alongside a more experienced colleague. I thought we'd know the nature of the allegation and the strength of the evidence, that it would be a considered decision. I didn't think I was going to be picking someone randomly off a list and bringing them in. To me, in this moment, it feels wrong – like we're paid muscle to do someone else's dirty work.

During training, when we practised arresting one another, it was all about getting the words right so that it would be legal. Now I am about to take someone's liberty away from them. It's not something that one person, in the normal run of things, does to another. And I only have a minibus ride to get used to the idea.

Gabriel is up first. Frankly he is the only one of the seven of us I would back in a fight. He's an ex-Royal Marine reserve – a military troop that only the toughest get recruited for. He's also worked for BTP (British Transport Police) before joining the Met so he is accustomed to making arrests and using handcuffs. Occasionally when we were paired together at training school practising combat skills, he would knock the pads flying clean out of my hands. He is a true gent so that would be him at 30 per cent force (he'd then take it down to about 5 per cent).

We direct Hannah to this address and park round the corner. 'Right, did you put a CAD on?'

Blank faces. She explains, very fast, that a CAD (Computer Aided Dispatch) needs to be created for any planned police operational activity. When a 999 call is made, a CAD is created by the police operator. When we go to arrest someone proactively we have to create the thing ourselves. It takes two minutes. It's almost like an incident ticket, a paper trail but also a live tracker.

'Cad 3784 TOA [Time Of Arrival] 11.10. Think of it as a safety net. If this goes bent, we call for back-up or press the red button, then people know exactly where we are and can come and save our arses.'

'Don't look so worried, it won't come to that,' she adds.

We've pulled up at an apartment block with a security door. Hannah whips out a firefighter's key and opens it. I feel awkwardly, apologetic for our oppressive presence as four of us stomp out and cram ourselves into the lift with a mother and child who look terrified. Then we're at flat 63. We all stand looking at the door as if expecting an 'Open Sesame' magic moment.

'Well, what are you waiting for? Knock!'

Gabriel raps on the door three times. No answer.

'Give it a proper knock,' says Hannah, then she absolutely pounds the door, which rattles in its frame. 'POLICE! OPEN THE DOOR!' she booms. We all wait. Please, don't be there, I think to myself. I hold my breath.

After the longest twenty seconds, in complete silence, listening for any slight noise from within, Hannah shrugs and turns away. 'Guess they're not in.' I exhale, before gulping in air.

We rejoin the others back at the van and drive to the next address. Some of the door knocks I sit out in the van as only four of us go at a time.

After a few unsuccessful attempts, we stop at a McDonalds to get some lunch. All still in stab vests and looking like a SWAT team, we're getting stared at by everyone – it makes it tricky to enjoy my Happy Meal. We chase this with a trip to Dunkin' Donuts next door. Living the stereotype.

Following one more post-lunch door knock, Hannah banging on the door so forcefully with her baton that I'm ashamed to see how dented and pockmarked we've left it, it's my turn. Simon Short, a tech whizz, has taken control of the laptop. He prides himself on being able to touch-type while maintaining unblinking, owl-like eye contact with someone.

'OK... let's see who we can find for Jess...' he says, flicking through the possible candidates, the laptop's case shielding them from my view. A spiteful glint comes into his eyes. 'Ah, this'll do nicely,' he says, passing me the laptop.

On the screen I see a big guy with a big criminal record, wanted for violent crime, GBH against a woman, well known for said violence. He looks massive.

'I've already put out the CAD,' Shorty says with an angelic smile. Meaning that it's locked in. We're going.

Brilliant, thanks a fucking bunch. I notice that my suspect's profile flashes 'Weapons'. He's bound to have a hearty array of blades in the knife block at home, I think. The home which we intend to invade and arrest him in. We pull over and four of us pile out of the van again, but this time I have to lead.

I approach the door with a little strip of paper in my balled-up hand, with his name, the offence, the date, the grounds. I don't trust myself not to blank and forget the lot. I'm going through the mnemonic (ID COP PLAN) in my head – the necessity criteria for arrest so that it's legal – but my mind is so focused on what's going to happen if he resists arrest that I can hardly think. Best-case scenario: he runs off and we walk away without life-altering injuries, worst case: we get added to his tally of victims. I take a breath, then knock as hard as I can, but absent-mindedly use my knuckles rather than the side of my palm. The others wince for me. I keep muttering his name under my breath as we wait. Silence.

Thank fuck, no one is in.

I soon learn that with these daytime arrest attempts this is the most usual outcome.

*

When we are fully fledged DCs in a few months, we will have responsibility for seeing every case we handle through to the very end – where there is a prosecution, all the way to court. This is known as Cradle to Grave. Right now though, we just get given cases to cut our teeth on. I get a burglary. There is a smattering of these allocated between us, including some fairly high-value thefts. Shorty is less than thrilled with his first case: the theft of a bicycle … wheel.

Our job description as detectives is initially to 'pursue all reasonable lines of inquiry, whether these point towards or away from the suspect'. But before you can do that, you have to work out how to use the police systems. The size of the text on the crime report system is ludicrously small. I squint to read the details and can feel my eyes strain. Maybe the detective magnifying glass association isn't silly after all.

It goes like this. My case started with a report of a stolen bike from a bike locker within a gated building. I took a statement from the man whose bike was stolen. Then I contacted the building manager and got a download of the CCTV. I watched the grainy footage of two grey figures, one in a flat cap, climbing over the enormous gate in the darkness and breaking into the building's bike store cage with tools, then ripping two bikes off the wall. Next, I took the footage to our digital assistance team, who crop the best clip and image from it and circulate it Met-wide to see if any officer recognises the suspect from previous dealings via the Forensic Image Management system.

Amazingly two hits come back on one of the men, both with the same name, so I can identify him. He's also wanted by City of London Police, who have CCTV footage of him stealing a bike by cutting the padlock with bolt croppers in broad daylight. I look him up on our system to see our history of dealing with him and find his address. We go to the address en masse in the van, but the woman there tells us he doesn't live there any more. She has nothing to do with him now, but provides a forwarding address. We go to that address; no one home. I arrange for a team to go there later to arrest him. Further intel checks show that this is the correct address but after several attempts at all hours we can't get him.

All of this takes for ever. I fumble about the police systems. Everything takes me ages to get to grips with, needing constant input from Hannah and Birdy. The thought that this is child's play and I'll have to process perhaps multiple prisoners for far more serious crimes than nicking bikes every day is daunting. Once we take and hopefully pass our exam in a few months' time we will take on serious and complex investigations dealing with the top hierarchy of crimes, and bringing in the apex predators.

The months roll by and my suspect has still not been arrested. Then, one day, out of the blue I receive an email from a solicitor who asks me why police have been calling at his client's house. I ask my suspect to hand himself in via the lawyer and to everyone's surprise, most of all mine, he does. He pleads guilty and finally — this is a year later — gets handed down a really minimal sentence and fine.

This was a slower process than anyone would have liked, particularly the owners of the valuable bike, but for me it is a textbook success. At this stage I have no idea how rare it will be for cases to go the distance when I hit my next department.

9

Practising on Real People

When I walk around the streets of Bethnal Green, often I am choked with memories of my time there with Josh. Looking at all our landmarks feels like pressing a bruise. There is the cafe we went to religiously for coffee every Saturday. I go in sometimes but now it's lost its shine. I feel saddened when the metal shutter comes down and isn't re-opened on the Spanish tapas place we discovered and treasured as a hidden gem. Turning into the police station each day, I walk past the bottom of his street. Glancing at the pub where we first met. He then flew out to join me on holiday in Bali just weeks after, which thrilled me; knowing him as well as I know him now, the spontaneous trip is out of character, which makes it all the more romantic in my eyes. I remember how full of love I felt for him and our future on all those mornings as we kissed in the street and went our separate ways for the day, coming back together more evenings than not. I sometimes think I see him walking towards me and flood with overwhelming feelings to the point where I freeze for a moment, but it's always a false alarm. I walk these streets alone now; he's moved on to a different part of town, and a different routine and rituals with another girl.

I miss him horribly whenever I stop and have time to think about it, but day to day, my new role absorbs me. Every week is full of firsts; the acclimatisation process is huge. And I feel a real sense of comfort living with Rachel and Paddy and Evie – all the more since I've lost Josh, and our dreams of building a life together and having a family. It's delightful to turn the key in the door and come back to their warm family life even though deep down I know it's temporary. They call me their orphan and refer to the house as the 'Orphanarium', especially since my cousin Lucy is staying with us at the moment too. We cook for one another, eat together, watch TV and laugh a lot, and baby Evie's gummy smile and hard-earned giggles light up my life like nothing else.

*

We're back in the 'fun bus', driving along the Bethnal Green Road, when Hannah spots a golden opportunity for a stop and search – another box on our list that needs ticking. She screeches over into a bus lane to take it. I see what look like two emaciated crack addicts, a man and a woman, using a public phone outside the Cashino. 'Dodgy,' she says. To me they appear to be wired and homeless. She summons four of us out of the minibus.

Police have the power to stop someone and pat them down airport-style if they have grounds to believe they have a weapon or prohibited item or have been involved in a crime. Sometimes, following a stabbing, for example, an area might be designated a stop and search zone and everyone within that area may be searched, but generally you need reasonable evidence. I can't see the grounds for stopping and searching these two. Being on drugs or destitute doesn't cut it.

As I look on, my insides squirm. What I see is that 'we' have stopped people because we don't like the look of them. It's plain wrong to profile someone as a criminal and I feel compromised even being there. I finally understand first-hand why some friends of mine can't stand the police because they've been hounded by them so many times in this way. As a privileged white woman I've never been stopped and searched but it seems like that would be different, say, if I'd grown up poor, in the 'wrong' area, or as a black or Asian male in London.

But Hannah's not exceptional in this. I've heard another officer say there are endless candidates, 'sitting ducks', for stop and search around Tower Hamlets. Mel tells me that in Croydon she and her cohort were sent into a multi-storey car park to stop and search tramps, which is a shocking abuse of the power. Lexi T's very first stop and search was a gent who was wearing no underwear and extremely loose, poo-smeared trousers – just her luck. She starts to refer to herself as a 'shit magnet' after this.

Through the van window I can see and hear the couple booting off that they're being picked on. They're right, they are. The woman throws her bag on the floor in protest. It's no small thing to be on the receiving end of this procedure. First, it's an authority figure acting on the fact they are suspicious of you. Second, it's an infringement of liberty and dignity, as they are detained for the search and their personal space is invaded in public. People always stare and think the worst when they see police doing this. It looks like the person in question is about to get arrested. You can imagine the lasting impact that has on someone's trust and opinion of the police if they've done nothing wrong.

We return to the police station subdued and glum. This is a prime example of box-ticking being so detrimental to the work the police do. Doing something for the sake of having done it rather than for the purpose for which it should be done. Shorty thereafter flatly refuses to ever do a stop and search again. I admire the courage of his conviction. In the circumstances that we saw today or those reported by the others so would I. Thankfully as detectives we won't be stopping and searching anyway. I can count on one hand the number of stop and searches I've had anything to do with in the Met. Afterwards, I bury what I saw and dismiss the procedure. At this stage I still very much feel like an individual in an organisation, and witnessing practices that jar with what I believe to be fair doesn't serve to institutionalise me, quite the opposite.

*

Each day we arrive at the police station having no idea what we'll be sent to do, which, Birdy tells us, mirrors the actual job. If Birdy sees an opportunity for us to experience something, he'll seize it and send us off, often at a moment's notice.

The first real interview I witness before I start conducting my own interviews is for a rape case. I can't quite believe I'm going to be privy to this interview for such a serious crime. I had emailed the DC from the specialist rape team, Sapphire, to ask if I could sit in before he arrived at our police station. We've never met before today, and he seems to think it's really novel that anyone would be interested in his case, but briefs me all the same. I read a transcript from the victim's interview, unsettled by the graphic sexual detail of how her colleague raped her. This really is the ultimate violation, as far as I'm concerned. I know that I would like to work in an area of policing that deals with hugely impactful crime so perhaps Sapphire is the unit for me.

I feel uneasy as we go to get the suspect from his cell and he comes out in a paper suit (all his clothes have been seized as evidence, as will this suit for forensic testing if this investigation goes further). I can't pinpoint exactly why I expected to find the man alleged to have raped a woman last night intimidating, but I don't. I wonder if this is something he's done before or thinks he can do to any woman he fancies.

In the interview itself he sits across from me. I spend a lot of time note-taking, not because I've been asked to do so, it's not even necessary as the interview is audio recorded, but to distract myself from how excruciating I find being in the tiny room with one middle-aged man grilling another guy about every aspect of having sex with a woman. The level of fine-grain detail that's being gone into paints this whole vivid scene move by move, as if the whole thing is being recounted in slow motion. The interview takes close to an hour. His version of what physically happened is almost exactly the same as hers except for one thing – consent. How on earth is anyone supposed to know who to believe? Someone is misremembering, misunderstanding or lying. But who? One word against the other. The lack of clarity makes my head spin.

After the interview I ask the interviewing officer how on earth the jury will decide who to believe? 'It won't come to that. Sorry to disappoint but this job is going nowhere, classic crap rape.'

What does he mean by that? It's the first time I hear that kind of phrase, and it will come to haunt me. Right now, I can't comprehend it. She has reported that she was raped to the police. That's a huge allegation to make, it's every woman's nightmare. He says he didn't. So... they just cancel each other out? No further action, no judge, no jury, no justice?

We all know the stats, just 1.3 per cent of 67,125 rape offences recorded by the police in the UK led to a prosecution (at time of writing). With the current CPS charging code and the way sexual offences against women are brought to justice through the courts, it would appear that near enough 99 per cent are so-called 'crap rapes'. I make it my personal mission to get to the bottom of this, but I immediately discounted working in the rape team as things stand.

*

I had anticipated less of a sink-or-swim approach. Just days after I witness my first real interview, I am doing my first solo interview. No one is watching to make sure I get it right. It's just me, the solicitor and the suspect.

My friends, when they ask about interviewing, clearly picture me interrogating suspects in a darkened room by the light of a single bulb which I intermittently shine in the interviewee's eyes. But the aim is not to get them to crack and confess, not at all. An interview under caution is the suspect's first opportunity to give their side of the story. This might be their only chance to spell it out before they turn up in court. My job is to establish exactly what happened and to make sure that my questions cover all the legal points to prove the offence or offences they've been arrested for, as well as possible defences.

At this stage I have no muscle memory of the preamble that we have to follow before every interview to make sure our approach is legal. It has yet to become a mantra I repeat on autopilot. In fact, the introduction and the technology throw me off more than the interview itself.

Every interview is audio recorded. But where all other police forces in the UK store everything in the cloud, the Met still uses good old DVDs – three, in fact: two working copies and one that gets sealed with a massive sticker at the end (which will turn out to be a further challenge). I fumble as I set up the interview on touchscreen, stabbing at the unresponsive screen. 'It's less responsive than the order screens in McDonalds,' I say, making a Dad joke to mask that I feel out of my depth. It gets a laugh once, so I use this exact line to break the ice in almost every single one of my subsequent hundreds of interviews.

My mouth is totally dry by the time I get to the caution. 'You do not have to say anything…' I rasp. 'But it may harm your defence if you do not mention when questioned something you later rely on in court. Anything you do say may be given in evidence…'

A little more housekeeping, then I ask my first big open question: 'Tell me in as much detail as you can about the incident last night.'

'No comment.'

Oh no, please no. Not 'no comment'. I can feel myself sweating. I thought he'd talk. In these first interviews the refusal to interact feels rude and like a personal snub. I have yet to adapt to the awkwardness of a 'no comment' interview. Every question must be asked whether a suspect talks or not in interview. The next ten minutes are excruciating as I rattle through questions, desperate to get it over with.

*

There are only two days during this period that we don't go into a police station but rather on an organised outing. On this fine, blue-skied day, seven of us are being taken to the mortuary to see our first dead bodies. I feel mild relief, as originally we were supposed to watch a post mortem too. Fortunately that got cancelled but there is still a huge knot in my stomach. Everyone talks about the nauseating smell.

The mortuary building looks remarkably like a residential redbrick house, which is disconcerting. We gather awkwardly and anxiously outside before Hannah leads the way and knocks at the main entrance. The door swings open and there stands an ageing goth. From top to toe he has long purple hair, a dog collar, a black top with fishnet sleeves and 'We are the weird ones' emblazoned on it, skin-tight black trousers covered in a silver spiderweb pattern and knee-high heavy lace-up boots with buckles and huge platforms. He's a cranky Australian who swears a lot and as we cram into a tiny office room he announces he needs a tea and disappears. I take in the room. There is a running theme going on: skeletons, grim reapers, poster quotes about preferring dead people to the living, the Satanic Bible standing proudly on the shelf. He pops back in with his novelty skull mug (I notice that his nails are coated in chipped black polish) and asks if anyone likes snakes, as he has his pet with him in the staff room. A few of us go to have a look. There is a fake tombstone in the tank with the little viper, and there is another guy in there watching the horror film House of a Thousand Corpses. Rick and I exchange a look of, 'seriously?!' and I try to suppress a smile. I wasn't expecting this, it's all a bit bonkers.

Our man is one of the pathology team. His knowledge is phenomenal, and while his tone is quite brash at times, he is sensitive about what we're shown and nothing but a professional. We start the tour and are asked to fire questions as we go. I ask a lot as I find talking slightly alleviates the stress of walking into every room never knowing what you're going to see and whether you will cope.

'Do you deal with children and adults here?'

'I don't understand your question. There's no difference, they're all dead, aren't they?'

I ask more questions, including one about the process of decomposition. He will come back to this.

We walk into what I would describe as the storage room. From floor to ceiling across each wall there are silver fridges, the ones we've all seen on TV. There is a drainage hole in the centre of the room. Then we go into the examination room, which isn't too dissimilar to an old-fashioned operating theatre. All the tools are laid out in preparation and there are towels everywhere (bodies leak). The tools are what you'd expect, with the exception of a screwdriver. My friend asks tentatively what he does with it. The answer, 'It's a fucking screwdriver, what do you think?' (it's used to attach different fixtures to some of the implements, as it turns out!).

Into a side room and we're shown various organs preserved in jars. In the changing rooms we're shown our man's customised black scrubs (he refuses to wear standard issue green or blue ones – he only wears black).

Our first glimpses of bodies are their feet. A row of them, one per shelf in the fridge. The toes are quite curled up. The ones we see are a pinkish tone of crimson and look hardened. Any plumpness of living flesh is gone. Maybe it's because they're old. One has a blanket, as the family, we are told, hadn't wanted her to be cold.

I feel panicked about dead people being treated with anything other than respect or dignity. They seem so vulnerable to me (I still think of them as people rather than bodies).

Then. 'Coming back to your question,' he's looking at me, 'about decomposition…'

The others look daggers at me. Here we go. He pulls out the bottom shelf and takes out a large full white body bag using a contraption that looks like a manual fork-lift. One bag is unzipped, revealing a second bag and another and another, like pass the parcel, until the final bag is opened, which is announced by a shower of dormant maggots hitting the deck. We didn't see the whole body, just the face, which had turned dark brown (he was white and his eyes are gone) and part of the leg. This man had been found weeks after he died and has no friends or family to claim the body. The smell isn't as bad as I'd anticipated, kind of a faint, sweet, mild Stilton cheese. Although apparently we've got off lightly as bodies on ice are very different to those found in situ, especially during the hot weather.

Looking at the blue thigh I ask, 'How come the jeans haven't decomposed?'

'He's not wearing trousers,' comes the answer and we all back away as the maggots are starting to wriggle about quite frantically, threatening to touch people's shoes.

Time to go. Those first rays of sun hitting my face as I leave feel better than ever. We all traipse to a greasy spoon cafe. The group is divided: half, like me, have a mere juice or tea; I manage a coffee, but people in the other camp are going all out on fish and chips, full English, you name it, appetites intact.

Later, reports came in from the other group's trip to the mortuary. The visit reaped experience of a post mortem to Death Metal, and the body of a woman who hadn't been found for a while and as a result 'her cats had eaten her tits off'. I was horrified too. Also, our man there allegedly sleeps in a silk-lined coffin.

*

Already, four weeks into being on borough, police school feels like a distant memory. But today is a day to go back for our Passing Out Parade. Today we'll join all the other police officers who completed their officer training at the same time as us. It's graduation day, except that where graduating from university marked the end of something, this feels like it marks the beginning. This is a day to commemorate becoming part of something. Last night, I spoke to Josh for the first time since my failed attempt at reuniting. I asked him to tell me that we were over for good, I needed to hear him say it to shake me into moving on. He wouldn't.

I graduated from Durham University a decade ago, and a memory that sticks in my mind from the day is for the state of my second toe, which judging by its violent purple colour and inability to take any weight, I'd broken in the early hours of graduation-day morning, stumbling home barefoot from a night out. Still, hangover aside, I tried to glide smoothly across the stage as I went up to shake hands with Bill Bryson and collect my mediocre degree. What little personal pride I felt about the occasion, my mum, dad and granny more than made up for. They loved the day, and I loved it for them.

My police graduation feels far more momentous. My fourteen classmates and I have made it through the role plays and early starts, the constant assessments, the sheer barrage of unfamiliar information, day in, day out for twenty weeks, and then onwards

into a development period that is one out-of-comfort-zone experience after another. In this time we've had to adjust to thinking
like police officers, to seeing risk and thinking legally and proced-
urally. When I think back to all those jobs I've had that so quickly
turned dull and robotic, I feel full of hope for the future. Now I am
starting out in a profession that seems full of possibilities. It's like
thirty possible careers in one. And eighteen months ago it had not
even crossed my mind as an option.

My mum and dad have come down from Cheshire for the day
and are all dressed up. I'm bursting with almost childlike pride
as I show them my new world. I see them exchanging glances –
they've always been cautiously supportive of my wild schemes,
taking the line 'we don't care what you do as long as you're happy'.
But now they can tell I really am happy, that I'm thrilled by my
new path.

The Met has put on quite the spectacle. There are fake crime
scenes for them to see, marching officers and a band, a horse parade
and inspiring speeches in the gleaming modern surroundings of
Hendon. In the auditorium, a looping presentation shows stills
from the training including a cringe-inducing image of me with
my mouth round a breathalyser, and a few shots that I now know
are true crime scenes and shouldn't have been included, rather
than the super-realistic training exercise my parents will take them
to be. The then Met Commissioner Cressida Dick, when she takes
to the stage to give the address to new officers, is inspiring.

We, the band of direct entrants, are the first ever detectives
to graduate at a ceremony like this. Amid the 300 or so police
constables in their police hats and white gloves, the fifty of us are
conspicuous for our lack of uniform. I recognise faces from along
the way – there's the woman with the five children. Great, she
made it through. There's the tutor I briefly fancied at Police School
standing with a clipboard, checking people in (awkwardly, I introduce my mum and dad). We never had a first date but he seemed
to enjoy meeting the parents. And there's Angus, beaming that he's
seen us all to this stage.

All Direct Entry detectives are summoned for a photo with the Commissioner, in front of Hendon's statue of Robert Peel (founder of the Met in 1829). A few among us clamber over each other vying to exchange words with our big boss at the meet-and-greet afterwards. I cringe as I hear one guy say 'I'm a Balliol boy too, ma'am.'

It's wonderful to see my classmates. We're buzzing to be all together again and for the day I feel nostalgic for the carefree police-school days and as light-hearted as I used to feel. But we're two down. Sophie and – the surprise of the day for many – Mia. I'd watched her become quieter and fade within our group in east London. She eventually told me she was leaving to go back to working for LSE and seemed so much brighter from that moment on, as if deliberating or waiting to break her decision was eating her. She had put a message in our class WhatsApp chat first thing to say she was leaving the Met and wouldn't be there but wished us all the best before promptly taking herself out of the chat group. I guessed she kept her reasons to herself because she didn't want to spoil our enthusiasm for the job or blight the day.

Nath is there but he's hanging on by his fingernails; the word is he's having trouble now he's on borough. He stopped attending the compulsory revision sessions for the NIE and said he couldn't do them as he wasn't taking his ADHD medication. In the light of this he's been sent back to Hendon, to join the Big Baby in stooge purgatory, as he doesn't have medical clearance to be fit for duty without taking his meds.

But how fit are any of us for what lies ahead? That worry is not for today. Sharing the day with my family brings this surreal new world I've joined into focus. I feel at peace. I've finally found my path and got myself somewhere that feels like where I want to be.

10

As It Gets Darker

November–December 2018

Each day, contorted in the cramped train on the way to work, I marvel at how many other people are already on their way to work at this hour. I often contemplate how unnatural it is, this crushing ourselves into each other's personal space and being transported deep underground – and how we endure this scrum. If there wasn't the implied consent, in any other circumstances it would count as an offence against the person, i.e. battery. That's when I realise I am starting to think like an NIE question.

*

I'm heading into the office, cutting it fine to be there on time, when a DC I've never met before stops me as I near enough run down the corridor and asks me to sit with some kids while she makes a phone call. I am surprised to see these two little girls. This is the first time I have seen children in the police station.

They're very cute, aged about four and six, sitting on the floor chatting quietly to each other, giggling and eating their way through a huge pile of vending-machine snacks. They don't seem phased by people clomping past in the corridor with radios blaring. I smile at them and they shyly smile back. Their hair is unbrushed and straggly, and one appears to still be wearing her pyjama top, but they look loved and well cared for. 'How are your biscuits?' is the extent of my interaction with them before the sombre and harassed-looking DC thanks me and sends me on my way.

Later I learn that their dad murdered their mum last night. He strangled her to death while the girls slept in their beds, then he too went to sleep. The next morning, he woke up, made himself a cup of tea and then called 999 to tell emergency services what he'd done. When the police cars arrived at the address moments later, he opened the door, piping hot mug of tea still in hand, and led the police to his wife's body in the master bedroom. These little girls still have no idea that their mum is dead and their dad, in a cell several floors below them, won't be coming out for the rest of their shattered childhood.

Days earlier we've heard about our postings. All the Direct Entrants start with six months in either the Criminal Investigations Department (CID) or the Community Safeguarding Unit (CSU). The idea is, we will do six months on one, and then switch. I'm pleased when I hear I've got CSU, which deals with rape, domestic violence and abuse on the borough. I joined the police to make a difference. What could be more worthwhile than protecting those who are under threat in what should be the sanctuary of their own home? This brief, heart-breaking encounter just confirms it.

We learn about Clare's Law that afternoon. This is a law that went through after Clare Wood was horrifically murdered by her boyfriend in 2009, and makes it possible for anyone to ask the police if their partner or potential partner has a history of domestic violence.

Unbeknown to Clare Wood, her partner had been extremely violent in all previous relationships, as is very often the pattern of behaviour where someone abusive is concerned. Clare's Law offers a 'right to ask' and a 'right to know'. If there is any relevant history or risk the police will arrange a face-to-face meeting for a domestic violence disclosure. What the person does with the facts they are told is their business, but they have enough knowledge to make an informed decision. Seeing the pattern cements the idea that the issues lie with their partner. Often just seeing the pattern, and understanding that the problem stems from the partner's behaviour and not their own, is enough to empower them make a change, whether that is to leave or to encourage their partner to get help.

*

With the National Investigators' Exam looming ever closer, all my spare time is spent procrastinating, googling 'how do I stop procrastinating', and finally, when I can divert from it no more, studying.

We have revision sessions to help us cram criminal law and police law into our brains. The sheer volume of theory, law and procedure we have to learn is vast but knowing the material isn't enough. We have to understand its application in any fictional set of circumstances that's thrown our way, and time is tight.

Eighty questions, in two hours. All the questions are tricky, turning on specifics of timing, or exact word-perfect definitions of a crime, playing the loopholes in various pieces of legislation. There are four choices for each answer, two of them extremely close so that you second-guess yourself. Some questions are just bizarre:

LAWSON, an adult male, meets EVANS, an adult female, in a bar. After a couple of drinks they go back to his flat. After a drink and some kissing, LAWSON becomes aggressive towards EVANS and proceeds to commit sexual acts with EVANS without consent. He first forces her to the ground and inserts a rubber dildo into her mouth, then LAWSON inserts his fingers in her anus followed by the rubber dildo into her vagina. He then encourages his dog to insert its penis into her vagina.

Considering the offences of Assault by Penetration contrary to s. 2 of the Sexual Offences Act 2003 only, which of the following statements is correct as to LAWSON's liability?

A LAWSON does not commit this particular sexual offence.

B LAWSON commits this offence when he inserts the dildo into her mouth, his fingers in her anus and the dildo in her vagina.

   C LAWSON commits this offence when he inserts his fingers
      in her anus and the dildo in her vagina.
   D LAWSON commits this offence when he inserts his fingers in
      her anus and the dildo in her vagina and when he encourages
      his dog to insert its penis in her vagina.

The Answer is D. The mouth doesn't count for this offence. In UK
law, rape is a crime that can only be committed by someone with a
penis ('penetrates with a penis' is the legislation). But with a dog?

*

My finger traces over the emergency red button on my radio – it's the
last-resort button if an officer is in a life-threatening situation. Once
pressed it automatically gives an officer twenty seconds of airtime to
shout for help in the hope that some nearby units will get there in time.

The feeling, coupled with the delirium of an entire night without
sleep and too much coffee, is not unlike waiting in the queue to go
on Oblivion, the scariest-looking rollercoaster at Alton Towers. I remember how I stood with my friends watching as the rollercoaster
painstakingly took people slowly to the top and ready to drop. We
could hear the clicking as the cart they were sat in ground to a stop,
the spooky voice booming 'DON'T LOOK DOWN!' as they were
held in suspense face down for just that bit too long – just long
enough to worry the ride was stuck – before it plummeted down
the vertical drop, tipping passengers face first into a dark pit full
of smoke and the utter unknown. It was impossible to tell if the
screams were terror or elation. Right now, I have the same coursing
adrenalin and the same nagging worry that I should call my mum
and dad to tell them I love them in case the worst happens.

If I was a uniformed police officer, being on Response –
responding to 999 calls – would be a daily occurrence. For us
trainee detectives, shadowing the uniform team as they blue-
light around London is another tick for Birdy's chart. My shift on
Response is also my very first night shift in the Met and it is fair to
say I am well outside my comfort zone.

My sense of dread started to bubble up inside me at about the same rate as night fell. My mantra at this stage is simply, 'Please no sudden deaths, please no sudden deaths, please no sudden deaths, especially hangings.' I have this vision of breaking entry into someone's eerily silent, darkened home, not knowing what to expect, only to find them dangling above the landing. The idea fills me with blind horror. I find it so bizarre that the role I'm in tonight makes this a distinct possibility.

If the awkwardness of my inexperience didn't already make me stick out like a sore thumb, the fact that Shorty and I are the only non-uniform officers at the evening briefing certainly does. We're in a police station we've never been to before, full of officers we've never met. I've opted to wear a 'covert' stab vest (goes under clothing), instead of the usual black Met vest, as I thought it would look more subtle. Dumb fucking idea, as topped with my pastel-pink jumper, I now resemble a friendly little cube with skinny legs and arms popping out from the side. I look like a lot of things, very special things, but a cop is not one of them.

We get split up and I am assigned to two officers and told we're going to join a team to do an arrest enquiry for attempted murder later on. WTF. I'd been hoping to be broken in with something slightly lower level.

We are briefed that he has a firearms warning signal, yet we won't be accompanied by any armed officers. Even though guns aren't a big issue in London I can't help thinking of the two police constables in Manchester who were shot dead by a wanted fugitive while on response. I imagine the guy we're after may have a shotgun aimed at the door ready to blow a hole through the first person to come bowling through. I don't want to be commemorated by the flame in the Hendon hallway.

We raid at dawn as there's less chance for the suspect to see the police coming and make a run for it. We set off into east London in a convoy of two cars plus a van to transport him back to custody once arrested.

Usually I can manage any situation – I'm adaptable and a quick learner – but this feels off the charts. I realise that here I'm at best ineffectual and at worst a handicap. And unlike during the day, where the Direct Entrants move as a group, there's no safety in numbers. I'm the only newbie here and I couldn't feel much more exposed.

But as we approach the outskirts of the estate everyone else seems chilled. Two of the guys in the car ask me if I want to do the arrest. 'It would be cool for your first one to be for attempted murder,' they say. They're being kind – this would give me bragging rights, which I've already realised are quite the currency in the Met.

'Very kind of you guys, but I think I'll pass,' I say.

It's still dark as we approach the council block, but the external walkways are lit up and cast some light on us as we get out of the cars. Each team creeps around to the second-floor walkway taking a different staircase. The first team has the door enforcer, the 16kg red steel battering ram known in the Met as the 'big red key' which can be used to splinter a door off its hinges if we're refused entry.

It's 5 a.m. and we're all assembled.

My colleagues bang on the door. 'POLICE. OPEN THE DOOR!' Then everything happens very quickly and is a blur. A woman in a flamboyant nightgown opens the door a crack. I just know instantly that she is the mum. She has a matriarchal kind of presence.

Someone asks if her son is in and she opens the door. Six of us traipse into the tiny flat – it's a standard London rented flat, white walls and wood-effect floor, but there are pictures on the wall; it's someone's home and the imposition, in the dead of night, could not feel more acute. Also, with six of us pounding into the narrow hallway, it feels very cramped. Her daughter is also there in her pyjamas in the hallway; she's about fourteen and just staring in a state of shock.

Our suspect's mum storms into his room and thumps the lights on. 'WHAT HAVE YOU DONE NOW, YOU BAD BOY?' she yells.

This isn't the gun ambush I'd feared. It smells like, and is, the bedroom of a chubby teenage boy. He's in his boxers lying face down spreadeagled on the bed like a starfish.

'PUT YOUR HANDS WHERE WE CAN SEE THEM,' yells my colleague.

Imagine waking up to this. He rolls around squinting and puts his hands up. He's arrested for attempted murder, which all feels a bit surreal in this setting.

Two men escort him to another room with his mother to get dressed so that we can take him back to the station. I can hear his mum ranting at him while practically dressing him and intermittently clipping him round the ear. He mutters 'It's nothing, Mum,' in response. His sister stands in the hallway, quietly crying and filming the whole thing on her phone. Over and over she asks, 'What has he done?'

The other officers have a scout of his room, taking a few items of clothing as evidence. They lift up his mattress and pull out a machete.

All this while I stand on the side-lines, trying to keep out of the way. I see his mum put his phone in her bra. Another officer notices too and asks her to hand it over.

Once the suspect is detained it all calms right down. He isn't cuffed – there's no need as there is no chance of him running off anywhere fast. As he's being escorted to the cage in the van his mum comes running out with an extra jumper for him and tells him to call her as soon as he gets there as if he's going on a school trip.

They stand and watch him drive away.

I was expecting someone terrifying, but he's just a boy – though the reality is that most of the murders in London are gang-linked murders. Kids killing kids.

*

The commute, hardened as I am to it, is beginning to wear me down. It's been seven months often of 4.30 a.m. starts now. On Monday I might feel up for the challenge, but by the end of the week, the cumulative sleep deprivation leaves me dog tired, more than the weekend can repair. It doesn't help that Rachel and Paddy have asked if I could swap rooms with the baby as she's outgrown hers(!), so now I'm on an airbed in the office. I constantly wonder if I should move closer to work. The average two-bed property rental in London costs more than my entire monthly salary in the Met. I can't possibly afford to have my own place and I'm not a solitary creature. Yet I've reached the point in my life where a flatshare with strangers is definitely not an appealing prospect.

My shift pattern, so hopeless for catching up with friends, works brilliantly with Rachel's maternity leave. When I'm on a late shift I can take Evie to a baby sensory class or baby gym session and an early shift allows for bath time. A bit like a second mum but without any of the guilt or responsibility. I'm Evie's first ever friend and she's one of the few of mine who I see nowadays. I know it can't be healthy to live in another family's home and life like this — I need to build a home life of my own — but right now I just don't have the time or capacity to start again. There has already been so much change.

Maybe, too, I'm still holding out for Josh. I can't quite believe that what we had has ended. My mind obsesses over the fact that he couldn't quite bring himself to say outright that we'd never be together. I keep looping back to that moment: was it cruel or is there something in his silence? I'm circling over it, as if I can make my tiny shred of hope grow.

One late evening, as I'm on the train back to Rachie's, I do what I have sworn I won't do, and text Josh. Amazingly, before the train even goes underground, he texts right back, and a couple of nights later we're in a Richmond pub, the one later used as the local in Ted Lasso, catching up.

He looks good. We're happy to see each other but both of us a little awkward as if aware of the immense power the other has to hurt us. Work's going well — his business is booming. They've been approached by new investors. But he's still with her, the new girlfriend. It's the elephant in the room and neither of us mention her directly. We are cautious as we finish the second drink and we know it's time to leave. Before we do he blurts out that when he thinks of the future he still sees me and imagines what our children would look like. I'm stunned. We hug goodbye for a long time, clinging to each other. I don't ever want to let go and sense he doesn't either; this isn't his usual aloof style.

*

The next evening I'm out with uniform again, a different two police officers I've never met before. We're cruising around Hackney with the radio garbling away. I really struggle to understand what's being said, this radio language and clipped tones is still so foreign to me, which is disconcerting as everyone else catches every last word.

Suddenly a call comes in that's rated 'I' grade, the most serious kind of incident requiring an immediate police response, within 15 minutes from the time of receiving the call to a unit arriving at the incident. Any number of the fleet on patrol can bid to take it and attend. The location flashes up on the car GPS system.

It's ours.

The sirens and lights go on and off we fly through the streets at break-neck speed. I'm thrown around in the back of the car like a rag doll, my freshly purchased coffee spattering all over the show. I'm flailing around, trying to cling to the seat in front to steady myself and plug the hole in the coffee lid that's pissing over everything. It's thrilling and nauseating all at once. I can't fathom how the driver isn't crashing every ten seconds. His skill is unreal. We move so fast there isn't time to let fear of what we're about to face creep in. The way the siren reverberates, and the lights reflect back through every window, makes the car feel like we're in a convoy of about seven police vehicles, all speeding as if their wheels are no longer touching the tarmac. I'm surprised when we screech to a halt, leap out and it's just us.

A gang of men are scarpering in all directions. They're legging it.

'GRAB HIM!' the driver shouts to me. Without thinking I launch myself at this enormous guy. As it turns out he's a beanpole, tall, wearing a puffa jacket and bulky clothes.

'STOP, POLICE!' I cry. I've got hold of him and he stops without putting up any struggle. I detain him and put the cuffs on him quick as a flash without thinking. I'm surprised that I have the muscle memory to do this with such ease from training.

I use the handcuffs because he's an unknown risk and has a big size advantage over me. And yet, I have no idea why we're chasing these guys – there wasn't time to ask in the car. This is exactly what you're not meant to do as a police officer. I am personally accountable for any use of my 'powers'. While running from the police is reason enough to suspect, I have only stopped this guy because I was told to.

I now gather there had been a gang stabbing in the area and that's what we were responding to. But this guy isn't bolshy, he's calm and deferential. I realise he's young, just seventeen in fact, and when I look at him closer, he has a kind face. I ask him for his name and we have him checked on the PNC to make sure he's not wanted. When I ask why they were running he shrugs and gives a shy smile. Then I perform my first ever stop and search, patting him down like an airport frisk, to check for a knife. He has nothing on him. I feel like saying 'It's my first time.' When I'm done I thank him for co-operating. He says 'No problem.' From jumping out of the car to this point only a few minutes have passed.

I can see here that, in the heat of the moment, a massive yawning gap opens up between how we are trained to behave, how I personally want to behave towards my fellow human, and what the situation demands. How many people are wrongly stopped in the heat of the moment and what does this do to their perception of the police?

This is quite a seminal moment for me, as I decide I won't follow orders this blindly again. This is not how I will operate in this job. Sure, the police attitude is to get the job done, whatever it takes, but I decide that I am going to make it my mission that every interaction I have in this job will be as positive as possible even in difficult circumstances. It's as simple as treating someone kindly and with respect. Holding on to my own values.

It's at this point I discover I don't actually have a key to hand to take off the cuffs. Thank God my colleague is nearby and seamlessly slips one into my hand.

We hop back in the car, beginning to let the adrenalin subside until the next nearby call comes in. Then we're off again, cruising around the lamplit streets. Response is relentless and there is no time to stop and decompress between calls as the intensity and frequency of them is as uncertain as waves.

*

To complete this weekend's 10k race I'd signed up for a year ago (I didn't make any plans nowadays), I had to dig deep. As I slowed to a stop at the 8k mark, the thought that spurred me on was that Josh would be there at the finishing line and I could collapse into his arms, a sweaty mess. This was pure fantasy but it powered me through. I vowed that I would put my fear of rejection to one side and swallow my pride one more time. I wrote to him in an impassioned plea that we try again.

No word from Josh as the weeks roll on. He reads but never replies to my follow-up texts.

I find myself crying in the shower in frustration about how messed up it is and how helpless I am to fix it. Mostly I just miss him.

*

The first time I meet DS Warwick Shandy, I wind up being gifted a string of four night shifts, one of which falls on my birthday.

We're gathered in our office room revising some law or other for the NIE when he walks in. I know who he is of course – he's been assigned to be my sergeant (line manager) when I start in the CSU – but only by sight. We haven't been properly introduced.

'I'm looking for Jessica McDonald?' he says. No preamble, not even a smile.

'That's me,' I say, holding up a hand.

'Right. I'm working out night shifts for the team. So you can either do a set of nights this weekend or the four weekdays first week in December.'

'Er... I can't do this weekend and first week in December's my birthday.' I also know that I'm not officially allowed to do these shifts as we're still in development.

'I'll put you down for the first week of December then. Good, that's sorted.' And he stomps out. It's so abrupt we all laugh.

'Hey Jess, congratulations on your new boss,' says Rick.

*

The first night shift coincides with my birthday. At 9 p.m. that evening I drag myself away from my cousin's cosy living room, with its log burner blazing. Although we're scarcely in December Rachael has already put up the tree, and rigged it to a smart plug so that on arriving home and in from the cold all you have to say is 'Alexa, turn on Christmas!' for the tree to light up and fill the place with cheer. I like having a birthday at this time of year and usually I'm childlike in my appreciation of the season to be jolly, but tonight, on the icy walk to the station, I can't help living in the past. Two years ago, on my thirtieth, Josh orchestrated a magical day for me. Knowing I love a view, he had planned the entire day around delicious food and drinks with all my favourite people at the top of various London skyscrapers and rooftop bars, starting with morning mimosas at Duck and Waffle and ending with goblets of red wine atop the Shard. I felt spoilt, adored and deeply happy. Now all I feel is tired and frozen to the bone. Even the smell of winter in the air doesn't buoy me.

Still, I'm curious about these night shifts. With fewer staff to deal with anything that comes in, I know I'm going to see stuff that might not otherwise come my way. I like the idea that anything might happen. And in fact it does. I arrive to find that we, the skeleton night-shift team (none of whom I've ever met before), have been handed a high risk 'Misper', a missing person investigation, from the late turn shift (2 p.m.–10 p.m.). They had received calls from a guy's girlfriend and aunt saying they were worried about him and that his behaviour was very out of character. They'd never had cause for concern before, but something felt wrong. They had no way to contact him because he'd left his phone at home and hadn't shown up to work that day.

In the UK someone goes missing every ninety seconds, and 320,000 people go missing each year. Of those, 56,000 happen in Met territory. When a high-risk Misper comes in you drop everything and work together – every report could be the first no-tification of a threat to their own life or someone else's and time is of the essence.

Our Misper is twenty-three and has moved down to London a few months ago from the north-east. He is known to be homesick, lonely and struggling. His girlfriend has been down to stay for the weekend. This morning he left the flat – she'd presumed, to go to work – leaving her a note saying he loved her. But later she found he'd left his phone and all his tools in the flat, and when she called his work she learned he'd never turned up. So where is he? Alarm bells started to ring even more when she discovered he'd trans-ferred a few thousand pounds into her account – his savings for the deposit on a house they talked of buying one day.

Searching for a missing person is a manhunt which can involve a CCTV trawl, full-scale hack of their phone, bank cards, Oyster travel card, social media, contact with anyone, etc.: anything that can give us a steer to track the person down and preserve life. Everyone is given a job as we race against time. This time, as we get stuck in to the individual roles which have been dished out to us, someone shouts, 'STOP! WE'VE GOT HIM!'

I feel a surge of relief, it had sounded so ominous. But as he con-tinues it's really sad news. He jumped in front of a train this morning. British Transport Police have identified him from what was left.

'Well, the good news is it didn't happen on our watch,' says the night-duty sergeant. Then, in case that sounded uncaring, he adds in a more sympathetic tone, 'You know, there was nothing any of us could have done.'

I can see his workload has been lightened. My colleagues seem desensitised to it, like watching devastation overseas on the news where the events seem surreal and one's empathy is dulled by distance. I know their detachment is an advanced coping mech-anism that comes with time and steady exposure to a whole raft of horror. But I'm heavy-hearted as everyone cracks on with business as usual. I haven't developed this level of resilience yet, and don't know if I want to. Everything hits me hard. I feel so sad for him, his girlfriend, his aunt, all his family and friends. All those who love him and will feel so guilty they couldn't save him. Every emotion is more intense in the middle of the night. I have to fight really hard not to cry at my desk.

It was naive but, before joining the police, I had only ever thought about what I would do and achieve, what I had to give. I hadn't spared a thought for what it might do to me. I hadn't considered the volume of serious crime exposure and the enormous impact it has both emotionally and psychologically until I'm in the midst of it. Blue-light workers in London experience far more awful things in a standard week than most people would within a year, two even. Do the maths on that.

I'm courageous but not hard-hearted. I can barely swim lengths of a pool on holiday as I have to stop and rescue every drowning bug, including enormous ants and wasps, in my path. Even at this early stage in the job I can feel it's taking its toll. I'm not detaching from all I encounter. I feel for all these people I deal with, both victims and suspects. Not having detachment in these interactions means I take on some of the pain, anger and hardship they face, which builds to have an eroding effect on me.

The clock shifts past midnight. It's my birthday. I realise that I'll check into work for my next shift before the day is out, so I'll be in work twice on the big day. I don't tell a soul, but pour myself my fourth coffee and hum 'Happy Birthday to Me' under my breath.

*

This is it, this is the day we've been building towards, the National Investigators' Exam. I head across town to the largest examination hall I've ever sat in, at the Olympic Park in Stratford. The exam is country-wide and only run a couple of times a year, so there are hundreds of detectives from all police forces and NCA (National Crime Agency)[1] investigators sitting it that day.

---

[1] The National Crime Agency is the UK's lead law enforcement agency against organised crime, often working closely with the police. The members of the NCA are civil servants who work on specific areas of crime at a national level, whereas the police have a far broader scope and enforce the law within smaller areas.

I've never in my life believed I've passed an exam at the moment we hear 'pens down', despite having never failed one. So this will be what it will be. I don't really feel anything before, during or after the exam. Usually there's the adrenalin spike before and relief after it's done, but I feel empty as I spill out with everyone else and head for a drink to the nearest bar, which happens to be a craft brewery. Comforting as it is to see everyone from police school, we're all knackered and the only chat is post-match analysis, which is an addictive yet boring activity. (Spoiler: we all pass with high marks except Tom, who fails as he hadn't bothered revising for it.)

*

Ever since I moved in with Paddy and Rachie, my stuff is still bursting from the suitcase, or in a tangled heap on the floor. I've finished the exam, I should be celebrating and getting in touch with all the friends I've neglected, but I can't face that.

Soon it's the weekend of our fake family Christmas with all my aunts, uncles and cousins, family whom I adore. This is usually one of the highlights of my year as forty of us assemble, crammed into the home of whoever drew the short straw of hosting, eating, drinking and awaiting the drama of the family quiz. But this year, days before, I'm dreading it.

I ring my bemused parents and burst into tears on the phone as I tell them I can't come for the weekend. I can go through the motions of my day to day, the usual tasks and responsibilities at work, but motivation in my personal life is completely gone and I can't summon it back. The thought of chatting to any single one of the people close to me at this merry party is horrible, because they would see I was a husk of a person, and I don't want to be seen this way. I've nothing to bring to the party, and I don't have the energy to pretend, so it's best all round if I stay away.

One morning, while I'm playing with Evie so early in the morning it's still pitch dark, Rachael asks me if I think I might be depressed. She gives me a piercing look as I hold Evie up, hand clasping her chubby thigh. She loves to help me press the button on the coffee machine and is the perfect little assistant as she also loves being up at ungodly hours of the morning.

'Are you sure you're OK? You just don't seem yourself. You look knackered. And you're thin, really thin, even for you. Are you eating?'

'Course I'm eating. I ate with you guys last night,' I snap. It's not escaped my notice that I look like shit, particularly the bags, like welts, under my eyes.

'You said you had that dizzy spell on the Tube after your shift the other day though. I'm just worried about you, sweetheart.'

Rachie's always acted like the big sister I've never had. Both in the best way and in the 'sorting out problems I haven't really got' way. She's a problem solver, but I don't want to be a problem. I've got enough dramas waiting for me at work.

'Really Rachie, I'm fine. I'm OK. Please just leave it.'

I brush her off, but something takes root.

11

Hitting Pause

New Year 2019

A good friend of mine has this wellbeing table theory: there are four legs, these are 1) friends and family, 2) relationship, 3) home and 4) job. She says that any one leg can be knocked out and you'll still be standing, but two legs out and it all topples down.

I've been through hard stuff before, worse stuff; I don't know why it all topples down now. I beat myself up constantly about why I'm not managing better. My room is in a state. I'm not looking after myself. Rachie is right, I am thin and pale. I don't bother with make-up or drying my hair in the mornings any more. I still haven't got round to replacing the phone with the shattered screen or shoes I wear almost every day that leak if it rains, and at this rate I never will. My reflection doesn't look like my own. I keep bursting into tears, but not because I'm sad, just numb and fragile. I've withdrawn from friends. I can't really face people because I can't handle anything beyond surface-level, functional conversation. And anyway, what would I say? How do you explain something that you've never experienced before? Something you don't understand, that has crept up on you despite pushing it down and pushing on? I didn't see it coming.

My NIE results arrive. In weeks I will start being a proper detective – still on probation but doing the job I've trained hard for, with a full case-load of real cases. I feel nothing, not elation, not anxiety, nothing.

I realise I need to hit the pause button. I need some time out. I can't explain exactly why but I have the strongest gut feeling that I must stop for a time. Just for a while, to sort myself out and get somewhere to live. I need to get my own house in order before I can help other people.

*

I request a meeting with Warwick, my new manager, and ask if, now that I have completed my development period and NIE, I can take some of my full quota of annual leave before I join his team.

'It's not brilliant timing, I must say. Why now?'

I say I feel I need to sort out some stuff in my personal life before I start. It pains me to have to explain as I don't want this to be his first impression of me. He leans back in his chair and twiddles his pen, stares at me. 'What's the problem then?'

'Things have just got... a little chaotic.'

'Boy trouble?'

'Well... kind of... I broke up with my boyfriend and I got chucked out of my flatshare, so I've been staying with my cousin...'

'How long were you with your boyfriend for?'

'Two years.'

I really don't want to discuss the details with this man or show how vulnerable I am right now. I can feel my eyes filling with tears. Oh God, I'm going to cry. I stare at a point high on the wall and will the tears to drain back into the eye and not roll down my face. 'I just need a bit of time to sort out my living arrangements... I just need to use a bit of holiday...' I stammer.

'There's police accommodation you could stay in, or the "Hyelm" (not-for-profit shared living, like student hall living), if that's the problem. Who knows, it might sort out the love life into the bargain – I met my wife there! You should go and have a look at it.'

By now I feel pathetic and ashamed. 'You know,' Warwick says, turning back to his notebook, 'back in the day, we'd never have had this conversation. You'd have been laughed out the room coming to me with a request like that. We all have things that go wrong at some point. But sometimes you just have to snap out of it.' This man is not going to grant what I need.

*

I try what he suggested and arrange to go to view both accommodation options. Mel and Lexi T come along for the ride. Hyelm is up first; I'm trying to keep an open mind despite seeing the gimmicky décor of the foyer; wall art of inspirational quotes, 'Live, Laugh, Love', 'Knock knock, it's Prosecco o'clock' and the like and Tube map-upholstered armchairs, and photos of girls hula hooping on the roof in the few promo shots on the website. It's like a hall of residence, cheaply done and impersonal. On arrival we're given a tour by a sweet girl who is brand new to London and seemingly quite scared of the city. We don't reveal what we all do for a living, it would make things awkward – you get a sense of who to tell and who not to tell. If you have just moved to London this could be the place for you, but if you're thirty-plus, and wondering why you don't have a proper home yet, it's absolutely not. 'Everyone's so friendly here, you hardly need to leave at all!' says the girl.

Mel and Lexi T are no help at all, sniggering and enthusing too loudly. 'Look Jess, all the free coffee and tea you want in the foyer – it will save you a fortune.' When she sorrowfully tells Mel that at thirty-five, she's too old to be considered to live here, I don't dare look at them for fear we all burst out laughing.

The Police Station House is an unknown quantity as it has no online presence. It's like a hostel, and feels like a cave. The guy on reception seems amused to see the three of us in the dingy reception. We're not laughing any more – it's bleak, like an abandoned old people's home downstairs and prison cell bedrooms upstairs, not remotely a viable option as a living solution. The only other person we see is a guy who looks like he's been booted out by his now ex-wife carrying a Tupperware box of microwaved food and shuffling from the kitchen to the communal area in his slippers.

The trip provides light relief and a rare outing with friends but no solution and no change to the feeling that I need to take a bit of time out.

So I email a Detective Chief Inspector I've never met before to ask if I can speak to her. It might be that in the long-term going above my new boss's head is not my best move, but I'm desperate. I like the DCI instantly – she's empathetic, with a calming smiley face, and she listens to my request, doesn't probe for details or tell me what I ought to do, but understands my need and within five minutes she's booked me off for two weeks' annual leave.

*

This break is long overdue. I've been so harsh on myself. Pushing myself on, denying all the signs. I didn't want to mess up this opportunity, which is everything to me. I have no history of mental ill-health and am still in denial that I'm unwell. I want to believe that if I sort a few practical things I've neglected and take some time out, that will fix it, whatever it is. I just want to rebuild myself to feeling normal so I can get back to work and make the most of it. I blame the heartbreak and not having my own home to go to. But ten days into my leave I've got nowhere. I need more time. I speak to a GP who seems to want to give out antidepressants as if they're sweets.

Just before I'm due back to work, I phone in sick. I feel so guilty, it's like I'm making a hoax call.

*

It takes a very long time for me to accept that I'm in a state of depression. Still, I barely tell a soul. I only talk openly to friends and am able to write about it like this once I come out the other side. At the time I'm so convinced I'm broken and will never be fully myself again that I don't want anyone to know. I don't want their pity and I don't believe I can be helped.

Depression is fucking horrible.

It's made worse as it goes hand in hand with hopelessness. One of the many tricks of depression is that you feel you'll never be right again, it doesn't feel temporary or semi-permanent, but like a permanently altered state.

Depression is a nothingness. I find the illness is characterised by absence: no interest, no energy or drive to do the things I used to do and enjoy, devoid of feelings. There isn't a specific trigger that would make it more understandable, but rather a creeping loss that sneaks in and saps everything away. I can't work out whether it feels like I've drowned on the inside, or whether it's an emptiness inside me which makes life hollow. I find myself thinking of a quote that is more meaningful now: 'ships don't sink because of the water around them; ships sink because of the water that gets in them'. Either way, all the feelings have gone. None of the emotional substance that makes life worth living can be felt. I can't even conjure warmth and joy from memories. I believe it's all gone for good.

Before I recognise I'm unwell, I blame myself and beat myself up for my inability to cope with life. I feel constant shame at how useless and checked-out I've become; sleeping in, sedentary and staring into space rather than up and at 'em.

The symptoms don't endear me to people either. They mostly mirror laziness and neglect as I withdrew from everyone without explanation, so most of my nearest and dearest were pushed away and felt rejected, perhaps taking that personally. The few who do still have the pleasure of my company find I am so hypersensitive and defensive that I snap at them at the drop of a hat.

Because of my ignorance and with no prior experience of it, I had assumed that depression looked and felt different from this.

I'm not alone: 60 per cent of the referrals made to Occupational Health in the Met are about suffering mental health problems. I too, get referred. It takes time but eventually I reach the front of the queue for counselling organised by the police. In the initial assessment there are a lot of detailed questions about suicide – whether I've planned to end my life and if I know how I'd do it. This is confronting and makes me feel like a fraud, wasting everyone's time, as I may be blank and broken, but I'm not suicidal. In the first session I feel impatient: I want to know how it works, how is the counsellor is going to fix me? I'm frustrated she doesn't tell me what I need to do. Why am I the one doing all the talking? The box of tissues on the table in front of me sits there like an invitation for tears.

But at the end of the session she shows me something that finally resonates with me: some scan images of a brain. The regular brain is lit up in neon green where it is functioning. Then she shows a second image, the sight of which makes me burst into tears. There is barely any neon on this one, the scan is dull. The lights aren't on and no one's home. Looking at this dark brain next to the lit-up, healthy one encapsulates exactly how this feels. The nothingness. She says that depression is like a brain injury and it can take up to a year to fully recover from a bout of depression – and that's without any relapses. That I was right to call time before things got worse.

Nothing prepares me for how unlinear recovery from depression can be. I head home to my parents, like a great big bird returning to the nest. They find me to be quiet, spiky and ineffective but otherwise outwardly fine. We're not a family that talks about feelings much – my dad is super-productive and keeps suggesting I'd feel a lot better if I did a bit more. True, if I could crawl out from this rock that's on top of me. Instead I spend quite a lot of time with my great-aunt, who has dementia. My mum and dad care for her, driving over religiously to look after her every day, and I stay and hang out with her, her humongous Doberman (which was being fed every few hours nowadays) and the little cat, collectively known as 'the kids'. We'd watch films together, the film choice growing more and more childish as her dementia rapidly took hold. She'd offer me a drink although sometimes the coffee machine 'wouldn't work', as so many things wouldn't in her world because she'd forgotten how to use them, or I'd be offered a cocktail of red wine and gin at 10 a.m. soon after her and 'the kids' had finished their morning fry-up. I adored her, she reminded me of Joanna Lumley – even in her confusion she lit up a room. While in theory I was caring for her, she was doing me the world of good.

So I stick with the therapist and she helps me to help myself until I can feel and function again. I didn't think forward while in the midst of it but I never once contemplated quitting my job. One of the first things I feel is sheer gratitude for the therapist's support and that of my family. I feel guilty for burdening them but mostly just so, so thankful they were there for me.

As an aside, everyone should watch the WHO video on YouTube, 'I had a black dog, his name was depression', a valuable use of five minutes.

*

Spring comes, and I find a new place to live. I move in with my friend Olie. Olie is a neat-freak and his house in Essex is show-home pristine – I didn't know that bleaching their ceramic kitchen sinks with a toothbrush was something people did of a weekend. Although I am not renowned for my domesticity, we get on brilliantly. We share a sense of humour and he's particularly funny so we're constantly laughing at some absurdity or other, which is such a tonic. In the evenings we binge on *Gavin and Stacey*, parroting lines, and hatch plans to make a TV show, start a podcast and get a puppy. I feel so at home there and embrace his routines. Olie goes to the gym religiously and body builds, so I too join his muscle gym, the legendary Ab Salute, out of sheer curiosity, even buying a tiny pair of fingerless weightlifting gloves. I've never been a fan of gyms but this place is different. Inside it looks like a warehouse that could host 'World's Strongest Man' competitions, which is intimidating at first glance but it's so inclusive and there is a strong sense of belonging. I love the atmosphere – something about the huge floor-to-ceiling mural of Arnie looming over us, wide-armed, biceps bulging, and the deep bass music pumping.

I feel like myself again; I'm back on my feet, dusting off and ready to step back in and give my all.

12

Welcome to CSU

Spring 2019

Even before I start in CSU (Community Safeguarding Unit), it's come to my attention time and time again that this department is a notoriously undesirable place to work. Whenever I tell any police officer in the Met where I've been posted, they wince or give a knowing smile. No one chooses to work here. Instead, it is somewhere trainee detectives are required to work as a rite of passage. The thinking is that if you can handle the relentlessly huge volume of prisoners who are brought in every day and the high level of risk attached to these cases, then you can deal with literally anything as a DC. In the Met, this department is as tough as it gets.

Previously, though, the trainee detectives initiated at CSU already had at least two years of frontline experience under their belts. It's unprecedented to have brand-new recruits cutting their teeth here.

The Community Safeguarding Unit primarily deals with domestic abuse across the borough. 'Abusive behaviour' is defined in the Domestic Abuse Act as any of the following: physical or sexual abuse, violent or threatening behaviour, controlling or coercive behaviour, economic abuse, psychological, emotional or other abuse. For the definition to apply, both parties must be aged sixteen or over and 'personally connected'. Domestic abuse itself isn't definitively a crime, but rather an umbrella term under which a whole host of crimes lurk.

Incidents, behaviour and injuries can look minimal on the face of it, but a statistic that's stuck firmly in my mind is that in an abusive relationship the abuse is likely to have happened thirty-six times before the police are called. Unlike the crimes in the Criminal Investigation Department (CID), where Mel and Lexi T are already installed, in domestic cases victims usually not only know the suspect but love them. Often victims will seek to protect the perpetrators. In every case you are trying to work out what happened behind closed doors and all you usually have to go on are two people's accounts – accuser and accused. Abuse is also a pattern of behaviour that escalates over time, meaning that the risk of harm needs to be managed extremely carefully. Of all the women murdered each year in England and Wales, over a third will be killed by a partner or ex-partner in their own home. Domestic homicide claims the lives of two women a week. Essentially our team is focused on murder prevention.

Also, it's been a few months since I stepped across the threshold of Tower Hamlets police station. Despite having shaved half an hour off the commute to work, this particular ride in lasts an eternity, as I'm feeling faint with nerves. I'm still a bit fragile from the time off and I had to really dig deep to walk through the door and come into work this morning. As I step into the main office the flurry of activity and unfamiliar faces is a lot to take in. I look for a familiar face, for Rick, Shorty or Gabriel, but they are all on different shifts. The only person I recognise is Warwick, my new boss, who I haven't seen since our first awkward conversation. I find a desk and say hello. He blanks me. The hours roll by. He doesn't appear particularly busy; I hear him bantering away, chatting about growing vegetables, but he has no time to acknowledge my arrival on his team. It's so long since I've been in the building, my passwords for the Met system and various programmes we use have expired. So for the first hour of my first day I sit waiting for them to be reset, pretending to be breezy and trying to look busy while feeling unbelievably uncomfortable. Usually at peace with myself, I've not felt this discomfort in my own skin since those few years of crippling self-consciousness during my late teens when I skulked around eyes down, shoulders hunched, believing everyone in any room I walked into was judging me. To pass the time I keep looking at a notebook and occasionally scrawl in it to look busy. I realise at one point I've written my name, drawn a few daisies, a dozen 3D boxes and then written 'FML' in bubble writing. There are four banks of eight desks in this office. Everyone is hot-desking, their desks a clutter of evidence bags, chocolate wrappers and chewed biros left over from the previous shift. Warwick alone has commandeered a desk of his own, by staking a claim with a handwritten sign saying: 'DC Warwick Shandy's desk'. Later, once I gain access to the system, I trawl through hundreds of emails that are now mostly irrelevant. It's unseasonably hot and as the day wears on, the office takes on a fruity aroma of dust, sweat and Gregg's pasties.

Oscar, the sergeant to our sister team, takes pity on me there, alone and friendless, and takes me under his wing. Other colleagues follow his lead and start to engage with me too. He's kind, interested, very funny and makes the effort to welcome me, which I appreciate more than I can say. Later that day Oscar buys twenty-four Magnums for everyone on our combined team. He makes a point of telling me that one has my name on before announcing to everyone that they're in the exhibits freezer. 'They're on the top shelf,' he says with a little wink, 'so nothing splurges out on them.' The exhibits freezer on our floor is used by the rape team and contains DNA, spit, semen, poo samples, penile swabs, aka 'knob swabs', and now, two dozen ice creams.

Warwick never gets round to talking to me; he stonewalls me that entire day. Coming back from a break for depression, I wonder if my time out has left a black mark on my name. I worry it has made him think I'm not up to the job. Or is it because he doesn't want Direct Entrants on his team? Or a woman? It feels like I'm being punished for something, but I can't work out if it's for my absence or my presence.

*

Now that I am a DC (albeit on probation), my day really does start, as Birdy told us all those months ago, with the question: how many prisoners – in his words, 'Got anyone in the bin?' Every morning the workload of the unit starts by checking the Night Duty Occurrence Book (or NDOB). The NDOB is a spreadsheet of all the prisoners our borough has in custody. Each entry gives their crime reference, the crime, their location – they could be in the cells at our station or spread anywhere around London – and a brief description of their circumstances. Given that the list is put together by the night-shift team, usually at about 4 a.m., these can be quite oddly written: 'DP [detained person] has thrown a cup at victim missing her however has followed this up by strangling her.' Or, 'DP has pressed up against female with his groin. Vic (Victim) was bending over locking her bike, there was sufficient space behind her for this not to be an accident.' Some details are superfluous – 'DP and girlfriend recently decided to buy a house together to get on to the property ladder' – but I struggle to re-member a day going forward when I don't see 'TTK' (Threat To Kill) on the NDOB. This is an indicator of how rife domestic abuse is. TTKs are so common that they aren't taken as a precursor to murder by any stretch.

From the minute a suspect arrives in the police yard, they are a ticking clock. They can only be held for twenty-four hours and I, as the investigator, must do everything necessary to complete the investigation, record and present my findings to a senior officer and potentially a CPS lawyer for a charging decision to be made within that time.

Once I have been given my prisoner by the sergeant in charge I head to custody – mostly downstairs in our own police station, although it might be anywhere in London where the suspect has been arrested and could even be in an entirely different force area or country. I collect the case paperwork and find out the time my suspect was admitted so I know what I'm working with and how much time I've got. Depending on the number of prisoners taken in that night and how rushed off their feet the previous shift has been, I might have twenty-three hours left on the clock, or I might be in single figures. I begin doing my investigation, following all reasonable lines of enquiry. I start by checking our systems to read about the incident and arrest before gathering all the evidence: the CAD, 999 call recordings, body-worn camera footage taken during the arrest, injury photos, scene photos, forensic reports, exhibits seized (such as weapons), taking witness statements from the arresting officers, from the victim and anyone else who saw the alleged offence or something relevant to the offence, such as doctors who treated injuries or friends who were contacted. Methodically every lead is followed up. Once I've got all the evidence I can amass in the time frame, I interview the suspect. Every prisoner is allowed free and independent legal representation, so I call to arrange that. The lawyer comes in, and I meet with them one to one to tell them what I've got. They then talk to the suspect. It's only then that I interview the suspect, which is audio recorded. If they talk I won't challenge them until the end of the interview. This is their chance to give me their side of the story, from which might spring many other lines of enquiry for me to investigate. My job is to get to the bottom of what happened.

Then I build a case file, write up my investigation and attach all evidence to a system we share with the Crown Prosecution Service (CPS). Next step is to refer it to a police decision-maker – a sergeant in charge of that shift. If it's suitable for charge I then have to call the CPS, wait in a phone queue (which can take hours) to speak to a lawyer, present the case and send the file. The clock is still ticking as we work towards reaching a 'disposal decision': either a charge, or no charge. If no charge, the options are NFA (no further action), RUI (released under investigation) or bail (still under investigation but with a specific date to return and with release conditions). I then need to go to the cell and release or charge my prisoner. If it's a charge I need to prepare everything for court, which is no mean feat. The suspect will appear in court the next day for a plea hearing and if they plead guilty a sentencing hearing will be arranged. If they plead not guilty the case will usually go to the Crown Court for a jury trial at a later date. I am the OIC (Officer in Charge) for every person I charge, meaning the case is my sole responsibility, and I must look after and prepare every piece of evidence until it reaches its final stage in the court. That might be years later. I do all of this myself, alone.

When I look around me, everyone is engaged in their own personal race against the clock. In police school and during our development on borough we had worked as a gangly team to get things done. Now, every case I work on is all on me.

*

By the end of the week Warwick assigns his deputy Ed to be the person I report in to. Already saddled with more work than he can ever get done, Ed doesn't look too pumped about this. But he wants a promotion to sergeant level and I, with my inexperience, will make a good case study for his leadership skills.

Ed is roughly my age, and calls me 'mate' excessively, as if he's worried I'll get the wrong idea about our partnership. Occasionally he cracks a smile and I see his face morph from worried robot back to human. Chiefly though, his default mode is suspicious.

While at work, Ed talks exclusively in a conspiratorial whisper. There are two key principles that he implores me to learn and he repeats them to me over and over. The first rule is 'trust no one', the second is 'cover your arse'. Every day, any time that we interact, he asks me, 'Who do we trust?' to make sure the answer is ingrained. I can't bring myself to play the game, so I just smile and let him supply the answer himself. 'No one, mate. We trust no one. Not colleagues, not customers. No one, got it?'

He must think I'm a really slow learner. But not trusting our colleagues seems to me at odds with the way the Met operates, and utterly different from how I think. Without trust, surely work already conducted by team-mates would be repeated over and over again? It's already clear to me there are not enough hours in the day for that, and I want to work as a team.

*

The team I'm on is one of about eight CSU teams, but the rota system, and the fact that you work wherever your suspect is in custody, means that at any time the office is full of DCs from all over the borough. Gabriel and Shorty are on other teams, and Rick is under Warwick with me. It's a running joke between us that Warwick hates me, but when Warwick is around, Rick keeps his distance from me to avoid any problems by association.

What strikes me most is how we are all on our own now. Before I became a detective, when I watched TV dramas, detectives came in twos. I know enough by now to know it was a naive fantasy, but in Line of Duty AC12 are a team. Any detective in charge always had a sidekick to test a theory on, the sidekick might see something the detective had missed, and together they would follow a case to resolution. At the very least, the sidekick world provide a bit of comic relief. Even in police school, we had clubbed together to figure things out; we're told it's best practice to interview as a pair. Now it's a shock to find that I work largely alone because there aren't enough people to do the amount of work we have to get through. I never anticipated that working as a detective would be as solitary as it is – such a lonely role.

*

My caseload quickly grows. Early on I get a prisoner, Danny Duskin, handed over to me from someone on an earlier shift. The interview was done, but the case file needed building. My job, now that the baton has been passed to me, is to get up to speed and write up the necessary details of our investigation in the system (COPA – Case Overview and Preparation Application), call the Crown Prosecution Service, present the case and get the charges authorised. It's my first time building a case file. Ultimately this will contain every single piece of evidence for the prosecution and the defence to use at court, all harvested by the investigator. It takes me hours and hours to navigate the system and put the file together. Nothing about the process of building a COPA file is intuitive at the first attempt, and everything is legally binding – it feels like writing a will and completing a tax return all in the one afternoon. At every step, I have to grab someone who is already busy with something else to ask them for help. My colleagues are kind, and as helpful as they can be in small bursts, but every single one takes one look at the case, sucks in their breath and says, 'Ooooooh, that's a big job.'

There are six charges against Danny from a two-week spate of attacks on his girlfriend, Ella. Danny had broken Ella's nose at the bridge, punched her in the face so hard he knocked out one of her molars, kicked her while she was down on the floor and made threats to kill her. When I go down to charge him, I see that he is massive, built like a fridge. In fact his sheer size is his strange upside-down logic as to why he couldn't possibly have caused these injuries. 'Look at the size of me. If I'd attacked her I'd have killed her.' I add a remand application to keep him in custody as he is clearly a danger to the victim, and phone the Crown Prosecution Service to request they charge him.

I'm so new I don't know how rare it is to get one domestic charge through the CPS, let alone six, I'm delighted when the CPS charges Danny on all these counts. Technically, this is where my involvement should end. It's not my case to look after as it should belong to the first detective who deals with the prisoner. But no overloaded DC comes asking for work back if there is a newbie muppet keen to take it on; I'm none the wiser that it's not mine to deal with and feel involved and keen to see the case through to the final outcome.

The next day, I head to the magistrates' court for the first time. I'm attending Danny's plea hearing and to make representations for his remand. After those months of going through the motions with bits of cases with Birdy, it feels to me like I am really doing the job I was hired for. In the dock Danny pretends to have an asthma attack and claims, via his defence barrister, that he needs to be freed to go on a religious pilgrimage. He's in rude health, and I'm calling bullshit on the religious mission. The magistrate agrees he should be taken to prison and kept there until his trial. Relief, a good first charge and a job well done for now. Of course this is not the last I will hear of Danny. Cradle to grave, remember.

*

As the weeks pass, I realise that we are flooded with serious cases mixed in with total non-starters that never warranted arrest in the first place. Today, for instance, after hours of work, I still have more or less what I started with: a man downstairs in a cell after a 999 call from his wife accusing him of whacking her with a hand-held corn broom. I've rung her for a witness statement but she doesn't want to support a prosecution and give a statement; I've conducted an interview with him in which he said nothing. There were no injuries, no witnesses, no previous criminal history and when the police arrived, she said everything was fine.

I start to talk Warwick through the case, but he cuts me off. 'That case was going nowhere, it was only ever going to be an NFA [No Further Action].'

'So why was he arrested if the only outcome was that he would be released?'

'Positive action. You better go and let him out.'

The majority of arrests don't end in prosecution (a charge). Of all the arrests for all offences in the UK, the proportion that do end in prosecution is 16.8 per cent at the time of writing. This figure is definitely lower for domestic crimes. Back in the day what happened behind closed doors was not viewed as police business. To correct for this past failure, the current Met policy for Safeguarding is that when officers attend a domestic 999 call, 'positive action' is taken to manage the risk. Among the Safeguarding teams this is often referred to as 'positive arrest'. It's true that for domestic incidents one of the ways to mitigate a risk is to remove one of the parties from the premises, and arresting someone makes this happen; however, arrest must be necessary. An alternative would be to ask them to go and stay with a friend or family member, depending on the level of threat they pose.

The decision on how to handle a domestic situation carries a high degree of responsibility for the attending officer person-ally. Basically the party line is that if one of these people kills the other, then it will be on the officer – and this fear-mongering leads to more blanket arrests than the Met can deal with. I and every member of our team have to deal with the consequences of this day after day. This is the result of Ed's mantra 'cover your arse'.

I trudge back down to custody and sign out his property. In the plastic tray along with his keys, wallet and jacket, lies the corn broom – aka the weapon he used to whack his wife. Before taking him out of his cell I speak to the custody sergeant and say I'm not giving the broom back. He tells me we can't keep it because we're not taking any further action. He has to take it home with him.

Bloody hell, it makes a bit of a mockery of the whole process if her husband returns home carrying the artefact he allegedly hit her with. I unlock his cell and check him out. When he sees the broom, his eyes bulge and he recoils, shaking his head. But the sergeant says he must take it home with him, so he carries this huge fan of dried grass out with him into the corridor, holding it out from his body and glancing at it nervously as if it's a mark of shame he doesn't want to be close to. When we are a few steps away from the police station's doors to the outside world, I ask him if he wants me to get rid of it for him. He doesn't need asking twice. He practically tosses the thing at me and shouts 'Thank you!' as he power-walks off in case I change my mind.

So, looking like an extra from *Joseph and the Amazing Technicolour Dreamcoat*, I carry this sheaf of corn back into the station and ram it into the first bin I see. It sticks out like a mohawk and remains there blocking the bin for a solid week.

*

It's hard to describe the full madness of the shift rota we work on – a mass of coloured boxes that rules your life. The shift pattern is predominantly made up of 'early' and 'late' core shifts. An early shift runs from 07.00 to 15.00, which means a 4.30 a.m. wake-up. A late shift runs from 14.00 to 22.00. Sometimes a late shift will be followed by an early one the next day, giving you hardly more than a few hours awake at home before you're due back. Night shifts run from 22.00 to 06.00, four days in a row. Every week you are due a spare day to catch up on paperwork during more normal hours, 10.00 to 18.00, and a couple of rest days – days off – that may or may not be consecutive. Weekends are no longer ring-fenced; it is possible to be on duty any hour of the day, 24/7. The default shift length is eight hours but in reality everything takes longer, and as you can only leave when the work is done or handed over, you're into overtime before you know it.

The shift pattern vaguely repeats itself every now and again, but it's so random that I cannot confidently agree to go to dinner with someone next Tuesday, or any single day of the year, without consulting it. The freedom of evenings and weekends is something I didn't realise I took for granted until it was gone. It's not fertile ground for an all-singing all-dancing social or love life. Not that I'm ready to focus on the latter at the moment, I feel too disillusioned with it all. Josh split up with his girlfriend weeks earlier and we got back together in the wake of that. It was too soon. I become a rebound for his rebound. The 'fresh start' relationship barely gets off the ground before he ends it abruptly by one-line text. 'I can't do this' … no further interaction or explanation.

But sharing a house with Olie is the next best thing. Whenever our hours coincide, Olie lets me download my day to him, particularly the odd and the mystifying. He relishes the details, and provides a vital reality check. Like today, when I had my first ever female suspect – a woman of my mum's age.

The story went that she was having breakfast with her two adult children when she received a phone call from one of her siblings with bad news. Her mother was in a diabetic coma in Turkey, had double kidney failure and was nearing the end. She would never see her again. The woman was so distressed that she lost control, howling, toppling chairs, smashing crockery from the table. Her husband ran in shouting at all the noise and grabbed hold of her to stop her flailing her arms and calm her down, not knowing what in the world was going on with his wife. She pushed him off and in doing so scratched his neck. At some point in all this chaos one of the grown-up children called 999, seemingly more out of concern for their mother than anything else. But instead of an ambulance, or social support, she got the police, and on what must have already been the worst day of her life, she wound up in a custody cell.

'Not one member of her family wanted it,' I say as I peer into the fridge looking for something that could resemble a meal. There is only one house rule at Olie's: no frying fish. It's fair enough. 'Her husband and grown-up children all explained she'd had an out-burst following the awful news; there was no history of an abusive relationship and there was no danger. By the time I went down to find her in the cell she was in such a state, clutching at my sleeve, begging, crying. I could hardly bear to close the cell door on her. She was my mum's age. Imagine if someone had locked up my mum on the day she got the news of my Granny's diagnosis!'

'Couldn't you just let her go?' says Olie.

'They wouldn't let me – I asked Warwick.' Olie closes his eyes and shakes his head. He's heard plenty about Warwick and, mildly put, is not a fan. 'He said "What if he [the husband] ends up dead and police had attended earlier and then left? How would that look?"'

'Such nonsense.'

'I know. Warwick said safeguarding's not so much what we're doing, it's what we're seen to be doing. But it's mad, we should be using the reasonable person test like juryies do, ask the question on the basis of what we know: is it reasonable to arrest? We can't just go round arresting everyone who has any level of domestic dispute on the off-chance they do something wholly unpredictable and uncharacteristically extreme such as murder a family member. Sorry! Rant over.'

'So what did you do?'

'I had to interview her as a suspect, with an interpreter trans-lating my questions. It took hours – hours of distress for her and her family, hours of paperwork, and then guess what, she was released. NFA. No Further Action.'

*

It's so much easier to be blasé about something you've never experienced. Forget spraying officers in the face with CS gas for exposure, sometimes I think standard police-officer training should include some time in a cell at a random moment during police school. With total luck of the draw as to how long trainees are kept in for, anything from a couple of hours to twenty-four, and maybe a few officers randomly experiencing a weekend remand for court on Monday. Just to see how it feels, so that every officer thinks twice about using this power. It's not unusual for me to be in a custody unit where ten, twenty, thirty, forty men and the odd woman who may or may not have broken the law are locked up in cupboard-sized rooms. Their crimes are only suspicion at this stage, but the experience of incarceration is very real.

*

Every morning you come into this job, you never know what you are going to be given, or where you will be. A crime might have happened in Tower Hamlets, but for whatever reason the suspect has been arrested in Notting Hill, Bromley, Scotland. They are taken to the nearest custody, but the case is ours to investigate. Wherever that person is, that's where you go. Head across town, find the police station, find the custody unit, find a desk space, beat the clock. I like the unpredictability, I enjoy the challenge.

Today is different again: I'm to be the police point of contact at a drop-in session for victims of domestic violence. Housed in a local public place to avoid any suspicion or retribution, the session is a collection of all the different support services available gathered in one place for in-person consultation – police, council, housing, social care, solicitors, IDVAs (Independent Domestic Violence Advisors), charities that can provide support. Here victims can source the exact advice or help they need immediately without a string of phone calls and emails, being passed from pillar to post or referred to some faceless organisation. It's a brilliant concept.

This one is held once a week upstairs in a public library or leisure centre on our borough, and is run by a wonderful smart, warm Bengali woman. She greets visitors at the door and gently refers them to whoever they need to see. I sit in my spot ready to do my best to help. The first woman I speak to doesn't speak English so her friend has come to help. She explains that she came here on a UK spousal visa but is being hit by her husband and that he has taken her passport and stolen her gold. As she can't speak English and isn't allowed to work, she doesn't believe she has the right to stay if she leaves him. I am troubled by this and don't know where to start. I assure her that her right to stay in this country does not rely on her staying in an abusive relationship. She can leave him and won't get deported. I take her friend's phone number to contact her later that day once I've had a chance to speak to someone on my team and work out what to do next to help. But she also needs to go to the lawyer at the table next to me. These cases are so multi-stranded.

The next woman I speak to describes how her ex-husband is harassing her. Harassment involves a course of conduct (two incidents or more) and the person responsible for it needs to know or ought to know the behaviour is unwanted. I feel on more confident ground here and it feels good that I can offer support and a range of solutions. We continue to talk and it seems the more I listen, the more she shares.

She must be in her fifties. She's a mother and a grandmother. She is Bengali and being separated from a husband in the community is quite taboo and judged by others, she tells me. I don't think she intended to open up as much as she did – like most women who speak to the police, she wasn't thinking about prosecution or even justice, she just wanted to make the abuse stop.

She tells me he's been coming to her flat and lurking outside late at night. So, stalking. I make a note. She's scared of him. She tells me that he's a bad man and that for the fourteen years they were together he used to deliberately hurt her. She wells up and her voice catches as she says, 'I know it's not rape if it's your husband.' She made an allegation of historic marital rape. It happened almost every night for fourteen years.

I have never felt more ill-equipped to deal with anything so significant. Tactfully, carefully, I confirm that she is talking about rape.

I tell her marital rape is illegal and she's brave for speaking out. I don't want her to realise she's shocked a police officer. Besides, it's only because I'm new: at this point I have never had a complete stranger tell me that they had been raped. This is the worst thing that anyone has ever reported happening to them – and I have only been told because of the job I do.

Scurrying back to the police station, the weight of the crime I'm now privy to makes my head feel it's going to explode. I keep muttering 'fuck' under my breath as I try and fail to process what she's told me. I look up the suspect and see that he's been arrested for rape twice before, once for raping his former wife and once for raping a family friend's daughter who was under thirteen at the time. He was never charged for either of these reported offences.

I ask Warwick what I should do next.

'Send the details to Sapphire. They'll take it from there,' he mutters, and turns back to his screen.

Sapphire is the specialist rape team, which, along with CAIT, the Child Abuse Investigation Team, has recently come under the CSU umbrella. As the new team settle next to us in the shared CSU office, we're been immersed in all things rape day in day out as they hot-desk all around us. They work much more as a team and over my head they discuss their day-to-day work with a dark gallows humour. (Sergeant in charge of a rape team: 'Big question – did anyone get penetrated last night?' and he wasn't asking about his colleagues' sex lives.)

While they might joke, what strikes me most is how much work they put into investigating every rape – every victim must undergo extensive questioning and an intrusive examination at the Haven – and yet how hopeless they perceive their work to be. I overhear two female DCs on the rape team agree that if it happened to them they wouldn't report it. 'What's the point?' On another day, debating which crimes could be legalised, one Sapphire DC says, 'I mean obviously excluding rape. It's basically legal now anyway.' The figures back them up. It's not news – the shockingly low prosecution figures for rape and assault have long been under public scrutiny. Nor is the problem that it is hard to identify the offender.

Stranger rapes, the nightmare of being grabbed in an alley, are such an infrequent occurrence that they make up only 2 per cent of all rapes. In fact they are so rare that they are not even dealt with by the rape team, but rather by a murder squad.

So now I speak to Sapphire, have a brief chat, click 'send' to deliver the details to the email address I'm given and that's that. They will take a visually recorded statement and I'm supposed to just carry on with my day. I hope beyond hope that at the very least someone really compassionate deals with her case. But I'm left with a nagging sense that I have let this woman down. She opened up to me personally and told me her story in the hope that I could help her, that something would change, and I don't feel I have done enough.

*

It's been a few weeks since Danny Duskin was locked up and I've considered it sorted until he stands trial. But today I've opened my email to find a message from a Prison Intelligence Officer telling me that Danny has been contacting his girlfriend Ella from prison, which is exactly what locking him up was supposed to prevent. Ella's mum had tipped the prison off that Danny had sent two love letters intended for Ella addressed to the next-door neighbour's house. It didn't take a genius to know they were meant for Ella, as he spoke of how much he loved her and wanted to be a family again, and dropped in her son's name.

He's also been phoning her using a fellow inmate's phone ID code. This is strictly against the rules of his remand. They knew there had been several phone calls of length. These were all recorded so I can get copies them if I launch a new investigation into witness interference to run alongside all the existing charges of violence.

I arrange a meeting with Ella to take another statement about these letters and phone calls. I can't help admiring her bravery in this whole affair, which clearly leaves her feeling guilty and conflicted despite everything Danny did to her. Ella's anxious but a very warm person and she and I build a good rapport. She wears her heart on her sleeve and trusts me, talking at a million miles an hour as dark and difficult details of their relationship come tumbling out. She tells me how he broke his ex-girlfriend's ribs, how she herself had to send her little boy to stay with her parents for a week as she didn't want him to see her black eyes. In his letters Danny had told her he'd changed, coached her not to come to court and asked her to put money into his prison account (which she did). Now, Ella hands over one of the love letters she received from prison, covered in scrawly biro hearts.

Although he's already started working on her not to, Ella wants to face Danny in court. The attack is fresh in her mind and she's angry about what he did to her. I have what will become a familiar feeling of helpless involvement. Until now I had believed that once the suspect was locked up in prison the problem was temporarily solved, but talking in depth to Ella makes me realise how conveniently simple that belief was.

*

The influx of new staff into our department not only brings more people colonising the already over-used desks, as well as different expertise and more manpower, but also the living legend who soon becomes one of my favourite people in the place: Doug Hudson.

I hear him before I even meet him. Where the general office atmosphere is a low-grade hum of discontent, and moaning about 'the job' forms the bulk of the interaction, Doug bounds in like a kid from the playground each morning. He's loud, with no filter, but kind and on the right side of brash. I think some find him noisy and annoying, but he's funny and full of excellent knowledge. Like so many very clever and book-smart people, he's also slightly socially awkward, but he either doesn't know or doesn't care that much.

We have our first ever chat about scraps, Doug's topic of the day as he sips tea from his Stalin mug one morning. Outraged that I claim to be northern (I am) and don't know what scraps are, he reads me the Wikipedia entry he wrote while at university in York. 'Scraps or batter bits...'

I jump in, 'YES! Batter bits from the chippy, of course I know what those are.'

But he's off. He recommences, 'Scraps or batter bits are pieces of deep-fried batter left over in the fryer as a by-product of frying fish, and are served as an accompaniment to chips. They are traditionally served free of charge with chips by fish and chip shops in the United Kingdom, although some places charge a minimal fee for the scraps. Terminology varies by region... In some parts of the north of England, they are referred to as bits or dubs; in the West Country they are known as gribbles. They can be found all over the United Kingdom, such as in Inverness, Edinburgh, Manchester, Birmingham, Cardiff or Leeds...'

Everyone has long stopped listening and gone back to their work, but he's started, so he'll finish. At the end he looks around proudly as if expecting applause. Time well spent. I was soon to learn that in the world according to Doug Hudson every day is a school day. No topic too random.

*

We get the alert that there's been an escapee from a nearby high-security psychiatric care ward (a place for someone to be detained rather than prison) while he was on a routine visit to hospital. Together we crowd round to watch the CCTV footage of how it happened. Split-screen CCTV shows a tall, lanky young man in a suit, loosely flanked by two much shorter, middle-aged women. We watch in tense silence as they amble from one screen to the next. They walk to a corridor and stop at the toilets halfway down. He goes in; the women wait outside. Here we go. Wait for it. We all know what's about to happen next. Inside he must be feverishly hacking off his electronic tag as quickly as he can. Outside the loos nothing's going on. Then he emerges slowly, takes a few strides as his 'guards' fall in with him, and then BOOM. Sprint start and he's off, legging it, and those long limbs are coming into their own. We all exclaim as we watch him zoom past all the cameras on site, blink and you'll miss him, his bases to the home run. It's quite mad viewing, like something from a Tom and Jerry cartoon as we see him dart across the still scenes. He flies across the reception area, the ambulance pool, through the car park, down the side of the building and the last time we see him he's running down a main road past a bus stop and out of sight. His burst of movement is so sudden and unexpected that no one gives chase, and then he's gone.

The footage we're watching is already twenty-four hours old. Now he's likely lurking somewhere on our borough and it's on us to find him – and fast, especially as this man is a convicted killer. The announcement of any Misper who might be a risk to themselves or to the public means your imagination goes into overdrive, and makes for an incredibly anxious time until they're found. A high-risk escapee makes this even more the case.

Our whole team is called to the briefing room. This isn't a usual occurrence. We're told the facts so far: there have been sightings. One is just round the corner from the police station. He was seen by a woman under the railway arches begging for 20p. This is a pathetic picture but we're assured he's manipulative and highly dangerous. An aggravating factor is that he was due to take his meds at 10 p.m. last night and hasn't, so a severe mental deterioration is anticipated.

For once we work as a team, all taking different jobs to cover all angles of the investigation. I go back to my desk to do some research on his background before I'm given my task. Hoping something jumps out from his previous crime files – motive, accomplices, family, grudges, etc. – I start to read through the case file from 2016. The day he killed his cousin. He had gone round to his aunt and uncle's house, as he often did, to see his cousin, a teenage boy of a similar age. The parents weren't home. The boy's sister reports hearing her brother shout, 'WHAT ARE YOU DOING?' before hearing his screams and a thud. She heard her cousin thud down the stairs and the front door slam as he left. She and her younger sister dashed to her brother's room and discovered him dying, his throat slit. Later in court it was revealed that he went to the house that day with the intention of killing his cousin because a voice had instructed him to.

Now everyone is given different tasks. It's a rare moment of teamwork and I relish it. Watching CCTV, contact with family or staff at the hospital, searching his room – we all combine efforts to save time. This one is hard because he was believed to be volatile and had no bank card or mobile to track.

The DI asks me to go through some papers that have been seized from his hospital room. I collect the two large evidence bags from the property store, full of a jumble of notepaper and torn scraps, letters that have been scrawled and scribbled on all over the back. There is a lot to sift through and all the while I wonder and worry if he's on his way to find someone and if the clue is buried in this scrappy pile on my desk.

Many of the notes are on children's A5 Harry Potter notelets; the border of each is adorned with colourful illustrations of broomsticks, wands and magical beasts. There are long monologues referencing his cousin and why he had to die. Then there are the names and numbers, literally hundreds of disparate names, phone numbers and places on separate scraps of paper. I start to put them all in a spreadsheet and team up with Doug to help work out who they are and where they are located. Many of the names are written on different papers over and over again, as if he's obsessed with them. Some are medical professionals from institutions he's been in all across the country. There are about fifty names that come up over and over. We decide to start ringing them if there is a phone number attached.

After hours of getting nowhere but working under huge pressure, we are told he has been found by police in Berkshire. And just like that, the hunt is over, the adrenalin subsides, and everything clicks back to normal, as if it never happened.

*

Over time I've realised that Ed has a tell. Without fail, when he approaches me and sighs, saying 'Hi mate' while exhaling, I know he's trying to sugar the pill before he lands in the chair, or crouches down on the floor next to me, leans over and lays a pile of crap on my doorstep.

Cases are not handed out using the cab-rank system, which would make for fair distribution, but rather cherry-picked. In the pecking order I'm the least experienced so I get what no one else wants to peck, mostly the no-evidence, arse-covering arrests which flood a stretched-to-breaking CSU, already beyond capacity with necessary arrests. Luckily I don't mind what I deal with at this stage as it's all learning.

Today I get handed a case file with a big 'E' on it: a boyfriend who doesn't live with his girlfriend but was at her flat, and tapped her on the leg with a baby's bottle, leaving no mark and no injury.

'Is the "E" code for easy?' I joke but Ed goes crimson, and I laugh. 'At least I've solved something today.'

'They can't all be crime of the century, mate.'

*

In an average week I deal with four prisoners, each case taking the best part of a shift to investigate, interview, charge or release, then I have proactive crime reports where I need to locate and arrest my suspect before investigating. I also have a case load of about twenty ongoing investigations to complete and deal with, including CPS requests for anything the prosecution or defence need for all the cases where I've charged someone and which are going through the court system at a glacial pace for trial the next year. The workload is overwhelming, more to do than can ever be done. There are always cases in our workload that involve people in desperate need of help, who are our responsibility, and yet we have so little control over the prioritisation of our time. If a prisoner comes in and is assigned to us then that is the priority even if that person should never have been arrested in the first place, and even if we have a court case that needs urgent attention.

If I personally feel the stretch of my untenable workload, so does every other DC I work with. It's an organisation-wide issue and one felt beyond the realms of the Met by frontline key workers nationwide. The reality is that with any blue-light work no one has any control over the amount of work that comes in, and the specific organisation doesn't have control over the size of workforce they have to tackle it. Cuts to public-service funding lead to recruitment freezes and the result is that there simply aren't enough people to get the job done adequately.

The department is so stretched that most people are grateful for us direct entrants as we are more bums on seats to shoulder the workload. But for a few this is a source of resentment. There's a feeling that I have got off lightly, swanning straight in without spending two years in uniform as a probationer. Uniform probation is a rite of passage and perhaps some see lack of uniform experience as an inadequacy.

Yet when I chat with Doug and Oscar and any other DC from the office, they all have these probation tales of woe. Very few people in the office buck the entrenched culture of breaking in probationers. A few decide that they suffered themselves, and they actively don't want that to happen to others on their watch. Birdy is one of those officers. Probation is usually a time of repetitive, robotic tasks day after day – unthinkingly following orders in order to become suitably subordinated into the disciplined service you have joined. During this time the new officers are often treated with contempt, as if they have yet to earn the basic levels of respect that employees, anybody, should be entitled to (but police officers aren't employees; they are 'Crown servants locally appointed', so maybe there is a loophole here). If someone can't hack it and breaks, then they weren't cut out for the job.

Common probation tasks include being made to stand guard on a cordoned-off crime scene for a solid eight-hour shift and perhaps beyond into overtime, in the freezing cold and the rain, unable to leave to go to the toilet or grab something to eat unless someone comes to relieve you by taking your place. Or a similar but sedentary job, constant watch on a cell, if a prisoner is suicidal. The probationer must sit at the open cell door keeping their attention on the suspect for the entire time, even if the prisoner is asleep. At best, it's mind-numbing; at worst it's much darker.

Everyone has their probation survival stories. Doug tells me that Dempsey was part of his probation, as if that should mean something to me. 'Dempsey! As in THE Nibbs Dempsey!' he says.

'I have no idea what you're on about.'

'Allow me to enlighten you. Dempsey murdered his wife and then severed her head, smashed it to bits with a mallet and then attempted to flush it down the toilet in their house before calling police to say they would find two bodies. But he botched his suicide and didn't die although his injuries were catastrophic, leaving him bed-bound in hospital.'

He rattles this off deadpan. I didn't believe the bit about the head but a google search reveals it's all true. Doug spent every shift for months and months on hospital guard, standing in Dempsey's hospital room, making sure Dempsey didn't escape or try to further harm himself.

Oscar's story haunts me more. Early on in his probation he was taken to the scene of a sudden death. It was a suicide in the woods, a young guy in his early twenties – about the same age as Oscar was then. Oscar had never seen a dead body before and his more experienced peers knew this. Once the body was cut down from the tree where it hung, Oscar's team made him examine the body. He fumbled, clueless and overwhelmed, as he had to cut the clothes off and examine every inch of skin for signs of foul play. He was then made to stand alone with the body in the dark woods until the undertakers arrived to take it to the mortuary. Then, he was told he had to be the one to deliver news of the young man's death to his mother. This is a more exposure to trauma than most people will come close to experiencing in a lifetime, let alone in a single shift at such a young age.

After he had spoken to her, the grieving mother contacted Oscar day after day asking that he take her to the exact location where her son had died. He wanted to take her, figuring it was a small thing he could do that might ease her suffering and unimaginable pain. His sergeant refused. Every day she asked and begged, every day he was denied permission, which he found agonising. Eventually he pestered the sergeant so much that for a quiet life he was allowed to take her. This is the sort of 'rite of passage' that everyone sitting around me has gone through.

But getting through probation, it seems, is a badge of honour in the Met. An attitude of 'I went through it and turned out all right' is rife. Over time the scars fade and are replaced with the belief that it is necessary to toughen new recruits up in this manner to give them the resilience and detachment they need.

*

Since I started I've hardly seen Gabriel – he's on another team. If any of my class from Police School were going to make it in the Met, I would have my money on Gabriel, and not just because he previously worked for the Transport Police and so knew a little more about what he was getting into. So it's a shock, just three months in to working in CSU, to get a group message announcing he's leaving. His text is hard to read – he cites sheer workload, and the impossibility of doing the job well. He thinks that we direct entrants have been set up, fast-tracked for cheap labour, given a punishing workload on the very lowest end of the pay scale. He signs off with a phrase that rings round my head: 'I genuinely hope you get as much out of the Met as it will want from you.' Maybe it's worth mentioning that Gabriel and Mia were the only two recruits from ethnic minorities within our class intake, and both have now resigned.

But he's not the only one who's already had enough. Word on the WhatsApp grapevine has it that Claudia, a member of our sister class, has also resigned, although I don't know why. Fiercely dedicated Claudia, who worked so hard at Police School. At graduation she was presented with the Baton of Honour, given to the most promising member of each class in recognition of their excellence, by Cressida Dick, who herself won the award as a probationer. Despite winning the prestigious prize, she has now left the Met and one of her less subtle classmates reports that she couldn't hack it. Whatever that means.

13

At the Hands of Men

Summer 2019

In Safeguarding it's easy to find the suspect but hard to charge the crime. Ed is standing in the office holding two case files, nothing surprising there – except that they're for the same domestic. 'Think of this as a parallel investigation,' he says as he hands Rick and me a case file each. 'Both have been arrested so they're both the victim and the suspect.'

'Remember, who do we trust?'

Neither of us answer.

It's Saturday afternoon, late shift, as the two of us trudge off across east London to the police station where the couple are being held. I have the woman suspect and Rick has the man. Usually there is one arrest at a domestic – a suspect and a victim – but I suppose if there is no way of deciding as it's one word against another, it's fairer to arrest both rather than get it wrong and arrest the victim (which happens). Rick and I review all the same evidence, then conduct our interviews separately.

My interview with Gianna is an audio-recorded suspect interview, and it's her first opportunity to give her side of the story. She is traumatised by the night, and talks at length about the incident, how her boyfriend strangled her and pinned her against the wall, which is when she scratched him across the face while struggling to breathe. She made a frantic call to her friend who lives in the next block of flats, asking her to call 999 as she thought he was going to kill her. The friend did just this and came to the flat to help her. The friend witnessed Gianna being physically thrown from the flat and her possessions thrown into the corridor. Between sobs Gianna begins to describe the abuse over the course of their relationship. I return her to her cell and make contact with her friend. Her story tallies and she comes and gives a statement.

Strangulation is an abuse behaviour a huge number of domestic victims report, leaving little visible trace on the skin. At the time of this incident strangling someone was more often put down as a difficult-to-prove common assault offence rather than attempted murder. Women *are* murdered this way. Grabbing a person by the throat and cutting off their air can also make someone wet themselves, pass out and feel like the life is about to be choked from them. Fortunately this terrible loophole was closed as part of the Domestic Abuse Act and at the time of writing non-fatal strangulation or suffocation is in itself a criminal offence that can carry a sentence of up to five years. I am delighted this is now the case and it fills me with hope that other gaping holes in the justice system when it comes to violence against women might also be addressed.

Rick has finished his interview too, a 'no comment'. He is a bit fixated on the fact that his suspect has the worse visible injury of the two (she scratched his face), but eventually concedes that there is a weight of evidence pointing to Gianna being the victim.

We call to check in with Warwick. I tell him we have all the evidence to charge, I just need to type up her account she gave in interview into a witness statement…

'You can't do that!' he interrupts.

'Oh. Do I just have the interview disc transcribed?'

'You can't flip a suspect into a victim!'

'What do I need to do?'

'You need to eliminate her as a suspect. Then, if she wants to make a statement, she can make it once she's released.'

'OK. I'll see what I can do.'

Poor woman. She's just been held in a cell overnight and had to relive the whole incident and history of abuse she's endured during this relationship. Now, to make her account official I will have to make her recount it all over again.

Gianna's emotionally drained and says she'll think about whether she wants to come back and make the statement all over again. At the moment her priority is where she's going to go now. She can't go back to the flat she shared with him. She can go to a friend's house but needs to collect her things from their flat before we release him. It's the end of my shift but I can't leave her high and dry. As she's been arrested, she has no money on her and as technically she's a suspect being released, no one has much interest in her circumstances. She's barred from the usual victim care on a technicality owing to her being incorrectly identified as the suspect. Custody will give her a pass to get free travel home but beyond that she's not really our problem. It's now 11 p.m. on a Saturday night and everything is kicking off on the borough as all kinds of live jobs, including a stabbing, are occupying the fleet of marked cars and response teams that might have been able to help. So it's on me, otherwise she's left at risk of getting attacked by him again when he's released on bail later.

I call back to the office and beg the night DS for someone on his team who drives to help me to help her. They send a team member in a car and together the three of us drive to her twenty-first-floor flat and help her flee from her house by night. We cram into the tiny flat; the views across London and the Thames are magical up here although the circumstances are anything but. I feel such an intense pang of missing Josh, no doubt prompted by watching her losing her home. We help her carry all the stuff that she's thrown into bin bags down to the car load by load, before driving her across to Wandsworth, south-west London, to the sanctuary of her friend's house in the small hours of the morning. The removal service has taken four hours by the time we arrive back at the police station.

Gianna moves away from London soon after and unsurprisingly never comes back to make her same statement all over again, which we need in order to charge him so he walks free.

*

Monday, early shift. I have a prisoner. I collect the paperwork and start reading through and doing background checks, piecing together what's gone on. On the surface this case looks mild – my suspect has been arrested for a common assault. He has marked his teenage son on the arm. Some particularly cynical colleagues might judge this apparent common assault to be a waste of police time. But the more I digest the details, the more risk reveals itself.

Reading through the notes I see the son has said he wants to kill himself and his dad because of the abuse at home. There have been some 999 calls in the past which have been shrugged off as accidental calls by the intimidated mother. The violence seems to be getting worse. In her witness statement, the mother says her fifteen-year-old son has taken to sleeping in her bed to protect her from his dad. In this instance, his dad came in unprovoked and grabbed her by the leg, pulling her from the bed, while the boy tried to fend him off. The dad pulled the TV they were watching from the wall and went to use it as a weapon but then started smashing it to pieces in the bedroom. Mother and son fled the flat and ran to a neighbour's. The neighbour had never met them before they banged on her door but describes them as 'scared stiff' when she called 999.

It's hideous to read the history and see the escalations, with the knowledge that we're only seeing a few jigsaw pieces of the full picture, but even this snippet reveals so much risk. To the mother, to the son, to potentially every one of his future partners.

The next day I find myself dealing with a father who attacked his wife in front of their ten-year-old daughter, three-year-old son and new baby. When I watch the body-worn camera footage of the police arriving on the scene in response to the 999 call, I see an officer trying to speak to the mum, who is clearly still very distressed. Her English isn't fluent enough to describe what happened so she summons her daughter over to interpret. The little girl perches on the arm of the sofa and translates what her mum tells her. She tells the officer that her dad pulled her mum to the floor and then started kicking her all over the body near where she had an operation to deliver the new baby. It's so sad watching the little girl diligently listen carefully to what her mum is crying and describing before very calmly and politely saying to a police officer not only what she has just heard but also what she has witnessed in her home, so they can arrest her dad.

Even if this father would never lay a finger on the children themselves, it is unimaginable how this indirect exposure to abuse and violence will impact their innocent lives. I think of my care-free childhood, mucking about climbing trees and building dens with my two brothers, the complete security of it, and think no kid should have their childhood contaminated like this.

*

I've already lost count of the number of times a sergeant might ask you to 'nip and take a quick statement', or, if they're really pushing it, to 'take a quick five-minute statement'. There is no such thing as a 'quick' victim statement for anything linked to domestic abuse. You're talking to a victim about their entire relationship history with a person. Abuse is a pattern of behaviour, it's never just a one-off incident, and these are traumatic events for them to recall and describe. You are probing into dark corners of their life, often enabling them to talk of things previously unspoken, and then writing the whole thing up as an official court document.

Today, I'm taking a statement from a young girl with her mum. She is very nervous and can't make eye contact at first. She has green, yellow and purple bruising all around her jaw – finger marks from where her neck and face have been grabbed and crushed, and, I later learn, cigarette-burn scars where her first love has put them out on her limbs.

This makes me so angry I feel a fire flare in me and stay on for hours making sure the statement captures everything. The moments in the job where you feel you could really help someone don't come as often as I'd envisaged, but this is one. The statement is key evidence and further down the line her abusive young boy-friend does plead guilty to the whole range of charges.

'I don't get it, why don't they just leave?' says one of my colleagues about victims of domestic abuse, a DC who has worked in this crime area for years. This phrase alone gets my blood boiling and it drives me mad how often I hear it. No one ever asks about the suspect's problem, that is, 'Why are they abusive?' The focus is always on what the victim, more often than not a woman, should do, rather than focusing on the abuser's behaviour, which is where the attention ought to be. It's the same with any abuse: sexism, racism, bullying – the issue lies with the perpetrator, not the victim.

Domestic abuse is such a complex beast that it is maybe hard to understand until you've felt or seen it first-hand playing out time and again. It has so many guises and exists on an enormous spectrum. There are huge swathes of grey areas. When does toxic behaviour, gaslighting and manipulation, cross the line into abuse in a relationship? When does the abuse become criminal?

Many people don't see abuse for what it is. It creeps up on them. It starts insidiously, with unkind words, criticism, control, arguments, flare-ups, interspersed with apologies, good behaviour, charm. It goes in cycles and becomes the pattern and norm of the relationship that often escalates into violence over time.

Often the abuser blames the abused partner for the abuse. 'They drove me to do it' is a very common explanation I hear. With their confidence and self-esteem at an all-time low, sapped by this unhealthy relationship, for the injured party there is no way to reason with the totally unreasonable. The abuser tends to see themself as the victim and sometimes the partner they're abusing does too. The victims of abuse I've met are often deeply kind, compassionate, loving people who want to help and save their damaged partner, so they endlessly see the good in them and make excuses and allowances for their bad behaviour, wanting to believe they'll get better. Deeply empathetic and understanding whatever adversity or trauma may have led to the abuse, they are essentially the abuser's carer and punchbag, literally and figuratively.

When I lived in Bali I had a relationship that made me realise how easy it was to pass off abusiveness as 'nothing'. He was Australian, significantly older than me, a very charming Peter Pan-type character, and although I never thought Bali was a long-term base, for now we were living together out there. It started slowly with the odd small thing that niggled at me, and I let it slide, but the shitty behaviour gathered pace and eroded my confidence. I soon noticed that he would erupt at me about one small thing or another before I was due to meet up with friends, an argument would ensue and then I'd be upset and exhausted and would cancel the plan to see friends in lieu of making up with him. Then we'd usually have a really lovely evening, and I'd be full of relief we were at peace again. 'I've never had arguments like this with other girlfriends,' he'd say, and I would rack my brain to try to work out what I'd done or said to warrant his explosive outburst. If I did still go out I would often find forty missed calls on my phone and multiple messages, but there was never an emergency or any need for the barrage of calls. Soon I found myself altering my behaviour to accommodate this possessiveness and avoid a raging fight, treading on eggshells and becoming more submissive – the arguments weren't worth the hassle. And so he started to call all the shots. It wasn't just the arguments that curbed my behaviour; it was the comments, and the belittling nicknames he insisted on calling me in front of people, which were humiliating. He made negative comments on my appearance, the way I walked, what I wore, the way I talked, poking fun at me for laughing, for over-talking; constant judgement. He'd compare me to his exes; I remember him once saying that if he put all his exes in one room it would look like backstage at a Victoria's Secret Show. In his eyes I was his 'little thing' (one of the many patronising nicknames). I had become quite socially isolated, as I knew my friends didn't like him – but they didn't see the good bits, all on his terms, when it was just the two of us. Sometimes, for a quiet life, I would lie if I was going to meet someone, and in that way, I unwittingly fed his paranoia.

One night I woke up and he was in the corner of the room reading my phone. Oh shit, I thought, now he's going to know. I was ready to come clean but he didn't say anything there and then. The next night though, we'd been out drinking. When we got home I headed to bed. I was lying in bed, in the dark reading on my iPad (ironically, about the Oscar Pistorius case) when he came in and put his face against mine and said, 'You're a fucking snake.'

'What?'

Then, still way too close, he shouted in my face, 'YOU are a fucking liar.'

I pushed him away and he shoved me so hard that I went flying off the bed and smacked into the wall. I saw red, and came right back at him. We had a fight that ended with him pinning me down on the bed so that I couldn't move. He was bigger than me and I went mad, screaming at him to 'GET OFF' so loudly that some girls who lived next door heard and burst into the room.

'Stop. Get off her!' They pulled him off and took me to go and sleep on their sofa.

The next day he claimed not to remember and told me he was sick when I described what had happened.

I've heard that so many times from suspects, that denial. But I had the bruises from slamming into the wall and his finger-marks all over my arms and wrists. I was sore, but mostly shocked it had turned physical.

I was lucky. For me it wasn't much more than a holiday romance, I didn't have kids or a house, I hadn't invested my whole life with him. Days later I booked a flight and left. I went home because I could — that was my privilege.

But it gave me an insight into how these things spiral. The women I see may wish to leave but this would be near impossible to do without an enormous amount of support and intervention. Late one night a woman came to the police station for help, with all her worldly goods in a suitcase and an injured foot and leg. She wouldn't tell us anything about who hurt her, or where she lived. Her foot was too swollen for her shoes so we gave her a pair of custody pumps, which I had to put on for her. Then we drove her to the hospital to get medical attention. But then what? Even if she can emotionally detach from the person, leaving throws up a huge number of logistical obstacles. Leaving could make her homeless. She could be financially dependent on him, she could have kids with him, she might be rejected from her community. Domestic violence escalates around the time of a break-up, so leaving might put her at more risk than ever if he hunts for her.

Every relationship is unique in its circumstances. When focusing on a victim I realised I needed to ask them how or what *they* want to improve the situation, rather than questioning their behaviour. Only the luckiest people don't know what it feels like to be in a toxic situation, trying to find a way through. Sometimes you can't even see it when you're in it.

*

Spring has turned to summer. Normally at this time of year, I would be leaving work to spend the summer evenings in a park with friends and a bottle of wine or outside a Soho bar or a river pub. Instead, I am scurrying across London on my Oyster card, navigating the capital's custody quarters. The first few times I go to interview prisoners at different police stations the custody suites always threw me off – the displacement, the daunting feeling of not knowing where anything is, who to watch out for, and being there all by yourself trying to muddle through. Everything is the same but different in each station – like a parallel world where everything is subtly shifted. But I come to love the underground bunker warmth, the jokes I have with the sergeants, the fact that, like hospitals and service stations (two other places I love), you'll find every kind of person down there.

*

I've just charged a man with the attempted murder of his wife.

She woke up to find him standing over her with a hammer raised before he smashed it down on her head. He hit her with such force that one of the claws embedded itself in her skull and stayed lodged there, snapping from the weapon as he raised it to strike again.

My role in this job was to review the body-worn video from the officers who attended the incident following the 999 call. Watching the footage, I see the aftermath from all angles. I have to decide what is key evidence from each recording, clip that bit and send it to the CPS lawyer to assist with their case. I don't know what each video is going to show before I click play; they're all linked to this incident but in no particular order.

The first clip I view shows the victim. She's in a neighbour's lounge in a blood-drenched white dressing gown, one side of her blonde hair matted with blood. How she's standing and talking is anyone's guess. It must be the adrenalin, I think, as I watch the officer on screen assure her that the ambulance is on the way and asks her if she's OK. Her first question: 'Is my husband dead?'

Another shows the arrest. The officers run through the darkened corridors of the block of flats. They burst into the flat where the attack happened with tasers, ready to come face to face with a raging man wielding a hammer. He's in the hallway, motionless and unresponsive. They point the red dot at his chest and shout for him to put his hands where they can be seen. He slowly does so, his face vacant. He's handcuffed and led out by two officers. The others stay and secure the scene. It's only at this point that I realise there is vigorous classical music blaring in the flat. He must have put it on following the attack.

Like a fly on the wall, the videos take me around the crime scene. At one point the camera stops on a smudged bloody handprint on the wall. Next, they find the weapon, the hammer, which has been tossed on the sofa like you would the TV remote.

The next scene I click on is an officer speaking to the occupants of the neighbouring flat. They report they heard nothing, dead silence, and then suddenly a woman screaming at the top of her lungs. They called 999 and said they would never forget that screaming. The young couple reiterated over and over that the walls are paper-thin and they can normally hear the murmur of conversation, but never arguing, and not a word spoken before the screaming. The victim had banged on their door as she fled down the corridor but by the time they got to the door all they saw was a naked woman running away.

In this instance the suspect isn't interviewed; the doctor in custody has deemed him mentally unfit for interview. When I arrive at the custody of our sister police station the custody sergeant tells me that for twenty-three hours he has not moved. He hasn't slept, eaten or got up. He has sat on the side of the bench, staring at the wall, frozen.

As we go into the cell it feels like the temperature drops a few degrees. As the custody sergeant tells him, 'You are being charged with the attempted murder of your wife,' he doesn't flinch. His nose is snotty and his eyes red, but I don't think it's from crying.

When someone is read their charge by the custody sergeant, they are read the caution again. 'You do not have to say anything. But it may harm your defence if you do not mention now something which you later rely on in court. Anything you do say may be given in evidence...'

His response comes in a thick Russian accent. The fact that he opens his mouth at all clearly shocks the sergeant as he jolts on the spot. This man had not spoken the whole time he has been here. 'Vot is the condition of my wife?'

On the bus home I sit in my usual spot, front seat on the top deck, and stare vacantly at the streetlight reflections through the rain on the glass in front of me. Questions I would never know the answers to churn around my head.

They both asked about the other. Did he care about how she was or was he worried that if she died his charge would be upgraded to murder? What's wrong with him? If it was a psychotic episode, was it right that he was sitting in a cell for twenty-three hours? Will he plead guilty? Will he get off due to diminished responsibility? Will he get the help he needs? If convicted, will he end up in a secure hospital like Broadmoor or a high-security category A prison? Will she stay with him?

*

It's just before the end of a busy shift, I'm emotionally drained and I have yet to eat breakfast, let alone lunch, when Warwick tells me to take a quick statement from a young girl who's come in with her mother. There is an assumption in our team that you 'stay on' duty, i.e. beyond the shift timing and into overtime, although theoretically you should be asked whether you want to stay or not. If you're moments away from completing something then it makes sense to stay and finish up, but sometimes there might be five, six, seven more hours of work to do before a case can be considered wrapped up. And that's before you consider the small matter of work–life balance, or having any life outside work at all for that matter.

Today I decide that no amount of overtime is worth it. I have plans. Olie and I have become like an old married couple except that we're not old, we're not married and we're not a couple. I realised that I'm lonely for a relationship, that I need to close the door on things with Josh so I can move on.

Olie is quite clear that I'm kidding myself. 'Don't do it, Jess. My aunt used to say, "Never go back." It never works.' He has a point. The last contact I had with Josh was a crushing four-word text from him that said 'I can't do this' and nothing more. We've not spoken since and that was months ago. I don't tell other friends as I know what they'd say but I don't want to hear it. There is definitely playing-with-fire potential here. But I ignore Olie, much as I love him, and his aunt, right though she doubtless is, and text Josh about meeting up. I need to hear the brutal truth that it's over, for ever, to squash the scrap of hope that I cling to once and for all.

So today I tell Warwick that I need to hand over a prisoner to the team on the next shift. He says nothing but just looks at me with silent rage, keeping up eye contact as if he had never heard such defiance and incomprehensible madness in all his life. Although he cannot actually make me stay, it feels like he is trying to intimidate me. The only other time I've seen an interaction like this is when my cousin's toddler, Evie, was told to stop stamping on her jigsaw puzzle and she just stared at her mum in sheer fury for an uncomfortably long time.

Josh and I have agreed to meet in a cosy pub, like the ones we used to while away the hours in when we first met. I feel sick as I walk to meet him. His texts to arrange our meeting were short and practical. I know he might be frosty or harsh, and the rendezvous might leave me feeling worse than I do already. He might be back with the girlfriend, they could be engaged... why did I come here?

I push open the door and scan the pub for a table where I can wait. But he's here already – he's beaten me to it, and is leaning over a pint at a candlelit table in the corner. He has a glass of wine ready for me. He looks up as I walk over and beams.

Oh God, I love his smile. I love him. It's so good to see him. The evening is like a flashback to a time when things were good, before I walked out on the relationship, before I screwed things up. We delight in each other's company and catching up, talking, laughing, till the pub kicks us out. As we dither over saying goodbye before we go our separate ways, he pulls me into him and kisses me in the street. 'Let's try again.' So no closure, but I couldn't have dreamed up a happier outcome.

*

But before Josh and I can meet again, I have a string of nights.

Tonight starts with a charming request. 'Jess – can you go downstairs [to custody] and find out if Kyle Fisher has jizzed all over his cell? Strange question I know, but I'm thinking of doing him for criminal damage.'

It's 10 p.m. and I've barely taken my coat off, but down I go. I ask one of the gaolers if there is a dirty protest situation in cell M12. He laughs, 'No, no, don't worry, it's contained masturbation into the trousers.' Good to know. I gather it's more of an adolescent rather than aggressive vibe in there. I don't need to see it for myself. The gaoler also offers, in a mildly impressed tone, that Kyle has had a whopping seven meals since his admission at 18.30. Few people find the custody food with no apparent use-by date moreish. Now he wants to speak to an officer.

I go round to see what he wants and speak to him through the wicket, the hole in the door. The stench that hits me in the face on sliding down the hatch is so potent I reel back. It's the smell of a neglected teenage boy's bedroom: a cocktail of smelly sheets, old semen and farts. He wants to know when he's getting out.

I go back upstairs to report back that the wanking hasn't caused damage to anything in the cell and to find out when and if he gets to go home. He's there because he called 999 to report that he'd raped someone but he's made it up. He's released twenty minutes later, having wasted police time, ambient meals and heavy-duty cleaning products.

Usually the first thirty minutes of a shift would be spent checking emails, but all norms go out of the window on night shifts. That's why I love them. The night shift puts me in mind of the on-screen camaraderie in *The Breakfast Club*: strangers from different teams flung together in the abandoned office block. This shift runs from 10 p.m. until 6 a.m., for four nights. The dimly lit atmosphere is calming as there are times of silence and nothingness in the darkened, empty police station, then a call comes in, and it could be anything. For once the usual pecking order of who gets to deal with the good jobs is abandoned. With just four detectives for the entire borough, it's all hands on deck. Team spirit reigns supreme and bonds us over this stint of shifts, all the while grappling with the fatigue in waves of delirium and exhaustion. The universal language of care for teammates is simply offering and making hot drinks every half-hour, drugging ourselves and each other with enough instant coffee to make it through.

While we eat our midnight Chinese takeaway dinner, everyone exchanges sudden-death stories. These carry high-value social currency, especially with someone new around who has nothing to trade, leaving the stage free for the others to showcase the worst they've seen. As I eat my chow mein I'm summoned to look at photos of a man who was cut clean in half, gutting him, after sleeping in a bin, the contents of which were put through a bin truck.

On this particular night shift there is a slow start and the biggest challenge is not losing my mind as one colleague waits for a CPS lawyer to answer the phone. He has it ringing on loudspeaker for three hours, reverberating around the empty office.

In the early hours of the morning the sound of the phone ringing is replaced by the sergeant watching *The Meg*, a film about a giant shark, without headphones and regaling us with the fruits of his Wikipedia prehistoric shark search.

Then a suspect is brought in to be interviewed for a double stabbing. I jump up. 'I'll take it!'

When I come face to face with the young suspect, he seems a bit unhinged. He's come out of his cell with a blanket wrapped around his head, covering most of his face. He's fizzing with energy, bouncing on the balls of his feet as if he's about to make a run for it. He seems unpredictable. I ask him to take the blanket off his head so we can talk. He looks like Justin Bieber. It's irrational and basic but I still kind of expect the awful things people do to have tainted the outside of them; it's a surprise to be faced with a teen heartthrob lookalike.

I've already gathered and reviewed a whole load of evidence for this incident. My investigation reveals he has stabbed his girlfriend, a minor, in the thigh while she was in his bedroom. A young neighbour heard her screams and came running to help. Justin then stabbed him in the leg too. The stab wounds are deep and both victims have gone to separate A&Es. They both made up stories about how they got the wounds, to the tune of falling off a bike and landing on a shard of glass. The doctors who examined and stitched up each of the victims observed that these stories were simply not plausible and in their professional opinions were fabricated to conceal stab wounds. I listen to 999 call recordings from each victim's parent, reporting what had happened, both of them naming the suspect and explaining that their children are intimidated and don't dare speak out about how they've been stabbed. The police who arrested Justin found a bloody knife in his house.

Justin says 'no comment' to all my questions.

There is more than enough significant evidence and very troubling levels of seemingly unprovoked violence here. I spend all the rest of my night shift, plus an extra few hours as the office fills with the early shift team, building the case file to secure a charge. I am on my knees after ten hours there and, having done everything I can, I pass the baton to the morning sergeant. I explain that it's all written up, so all that needs to happen now is for someone to skim though my write-up of the facts of the offence and call the CPS to have him charged and remanded for double GBH.

Roll on the next night after a day sleeping, fully transitioning into a nocturnal creature. On arrival we, the hoodie-clad night-shifters, all greet each other and tally the hours of daytime sleep we achieved. I'm amazed at how some teammates survive on snatches of sleep between night shifts, usually those with kids who want to see them, or people who really struggle to change their circadian rhythm on demand. Never have I appreciated the gift of the ability to sleep anywhere, anytime, more than while I am on nights.

I log in and learn that Justin was released. NFA – No Further Action. The reason being: no victims, no crime. I am furious, incensed, incredulous. I can feel my pulse throbbing in my head. How can someone who stabs two children, causing them both to attend A&E, be let out, case closed? I stew on it all night and can't let it go. When the shifts change over the next morning I approach Warwick to raise concerns about the case. I felt the CPS's decision not to charge needed to be challenged as there was so much evidence and this suspect posed a real danger. I volunteer to take it on, more than happy to do whatever it takes as I can feel in my gut that letting someone who's stabbed two young people walk free is a disaster waiting to happen.

Warwick tells me caring about this isn't my remit. He mansplains, with actions, that this case is gone, done and dusted. He stands up from his chair, pretends to bat a ball away with force, raising a hand to his eyes and squinting into the distance, then taking an over-exaggerated step away and doing the action of washing his hands of it. 'You've done your bit. If he kills her, or anyone else, it wouldn't come back at you. It's not your job to have concerns about this.' As I walk away I feel as if my head is going to explode.

*

The Crown Prosecution Service: every case we deal with, we come up against this wall. The detectives do the legwork, present the case to them and the Crown Prosecution Service (a separate entity from the police within the criminal justice system) assesses whether to charge or not. Essentially the CPS is a bank of lawyers, working mostly from home or from an office in London called Petty France, who assess whether or not a case is strong enough to be tried. It's very old-school: we phone in and present the case, they make the decision.

There is a glaring problem. The two organisations' objectives are not aligned. The Met is victim-focused: our aim is to achieve the best outcome in the pursuit of justice and in support of victims, in their best interests. The CPS is success-focused: when making a charging decision, the CPS look for there to be a 'realistic prospect of conviction'.

Now consider domestic crime: it's complex and nuanced, there are mostly no witnesses, no CCTV or digital evidence as it's behind closed doors, no forensics as they live together. It often comes down to one person's word against the other. One word against the other does not offer the CPS a 'realistic prospect of conviction' – it could go either way. So the CPS refuses to charge the vast majority of safeguarding cases, especially as they could adversely affect their success at court statistics.

The result? A dysfunctional system that deprives the vast majority of victims of domestic crimes and rape of access to justice. As the bulk of those victims are women, it's hard not to feel that CPS's charging standards are inherently misogynistic. One in five of all crimes dealt with by the CPS involves violence against women and girls (VAWG), so this is no small oversight – thousands of women each year denied access to justice and left scared of what might happen next.

*

Driving through Dalston at 3 a.m., I stare out of the police-car window at all these people living their lives, spilling out of bars, laughing with friends. I watch, removed from it all, feeling pangs of nostalgia as we drive by. I was once that social animal. I pine for my old life, the normal London life that feels so distant now. When I was in the hole of depression I withdrew from everyone. I didn't go out, make contact, or share why I stopped being there. Now it feels too daunting to rebuild that life; it feels permanently lost.

*

The most serious, violent, high-risk, maddest stuff in east London happens at night. Tonight we're at a crime scene – a rarity when you're investigating domestic violence. It tends to be more 'he said she said' – one person's word against the other – plus any injuries and maybe people who've overheard. But tonight there is a man fighting for his life in hospital who's told us that some strangers stabbed him in the neck outside his flat. Officers who attended the 999 call state this couldn't have happened as he described it as there is no blood from the near-catastrophic wound anywhere outside the flat. They have arrested the victim's girlfriend as they believe she attacked him in the flat. Everyone here is obsessing over the fact that she's covered in shit. The blood and the near-fatal stab wound are par for the course, the faeces not so much.

Anytime somewhere needs to be preserved as a crime scene, an officer (usually a probationer) stays at the scene to guard and monitor who goes in and out. When we, Russell, the sergeant who's in charge tonight, Ed and I arrive, there is a blank-faced policewoman sitting on a chair outside the front door to the flat. She tells us that it's a sealed crime scene, no one has been in since the paramedics whisked him away to A&E and the girlfriend was arrested.

I feel we should be wearing full barrier clothing, but we're just in blue gloves. Russell eases the door open, pushing it near the hinge so as to avoid destroying any forensic opportunities on the handle.

We tiptoe in. The first two metres of floor behind the front door are completely normal and then there's a long, unbroken smear of blood, the width of a grown man, that runs the length of the narrow hallway (we should be wearing booties over our shoes). It's an unsubtle clue which we awkwardly straddle, trying not to dip our feet in at any point or slip. We reach the bedroom, where we all stop and stare at the blood-drenched pillow on the right side of the double bed. 'Looks like she stabbed him while he was lying in bed,' says Ed. It's clear that from here the wide blood smear we've been following is where he dragged himself away along the floor before collapsing in the hallway, to be found unconscious by the paramedics.

The flat is a typical one-bed in London, small, with open-plan living area in which there is nothing of note, perfectly clean, no blood. In the kitchen I find a little thin screwdriver, like one you might get in a posh cracker, on the draining board. 'She could have stabbed him with this.' I point at it.

'No, Jess,' the other two say in a condescending unison.

'Do we know what the puncture wound looked like?' I'm a bit offended as I didn't think it was the dumbest suggestion.

'Probably not like he fell on a toy screwdriver,' Russell smirks and Ed chuckles.

We've seen enough to know exactly where he was stabbed and that he is telling us a cover story. Russell decides we should leave as we don't want to contaminate or disrupt the crime scene. A forensic team will soon arrive to take photos and thoroughly examine the place.

About an hour later someone at the hospital reports in, stating that the puncture wound is small but deep. 'Must have been caused by something like a meat skewer or screwdriver,' they hypothesise. I say nothing. I see Russell and Ed exchange a look.

We hand over to the early shift and when we resume that night, we learn that she was released and no further action will be taken. 'How can that be?' I ask, outraged. 'There is no way anyone else could have done it.' The CPS state there is not enough evidence to charge as no one is explicitly saying she did it. She was the only one there, she stabbed him, she washed the weapon and she never got prosecuted. No victim, no crime.

*

More emergency workers die on the way home from work (or by suicide) than in the line of duty. A statistic I found weird until I experienced the reality of post-nights exhaustion first-hand.

It's 05.59 and I'm waiting for the first Tube to take me to the train station, where I'll wait impatiently for the first train to take me back to Essex.

A thirteen-minute wait for the tube... thirteen minutes! I want to cry, I want to laugh. I can't process what I've seen and done tonight. I won't tell anyone what I saw because I can't be bothered with their questions and they'll never understand it anyway.

I've had too much coffee in the last few hours and feel wired and exhausted in crashing waves. I keep having the urge to belt out certain songs aloud at the top of my voice, mostly my favourite show tunes, power ballads or something that was on the radio a few hours ago in the office and is now lodged in my brain on a loop. The sleep deprivation feels like a flirtation and dance with madness. I just want to get to my bed and the two-hour pilgrimage feels intense. I have moments of paranoia, not unlike the fear of a really bad hangover. I think about being pushed in front of the Tube and pre-emptively adapt my stance, sideways with legs spread wider apart. 'Good luck shoving me over the edge now.' There are about three people there and no one closer than ten metres away. I'm agitated and feel like I could lose it and even attack someone at the slightest irritation. I start pacing the platform.

I walk past a med student or junior doctor in scrubs who smells like a musty shared student house —those days of learning to be independent, thinking you could get away with leaving soggy clothes in the washing-machine drum, believing they won't smell bad when they dry. All this staying awake wreaks havoc with my heightened senses.

On the Tube I spend the journey looking down intensely at a dark spot on my white trainers for three minutes as my head swims. 'It's only tea!' In my delirium I've been convinced it's a bloodstain from the crime scene, and I'm perplexed as to how it would have got onto that bit of my shoe.

Done with being possessed like Lady Macbeth, I arrive at Stratford and pelt to the platform. I'm obsessed with getting home to my bed. I miss the first train and stand shivering on the freezing dark platform for the longest twenty mins. It's too early for a direct train so I have to swap and the connection time is barely possible, even at a sprint.

Legging it to catch my connecting train, I hear frantic footsteps behind me. A girl still out from the night before in a tiny dress yells, 'HOLD THE DOOR FOR ME, CHICK!' We laugh dementedly as we thud and clack across the railway bridge – it feels so good and I realise it's the first time I've laughed in twenty-four hours.

When I finally get home the elation of Rosie, Olie's brand-new French Bulldog puppy, almost brings me to tears. The bat-eared baby has flattened her ears back in sheer delight at seeing me. She pays no mind to the state of me and is grunting and wiggling with joy behind her baby-gated zone of the kitchen. I kneel on the floor and she clambers onto me, delighted I'm there and desperate to lick my face and nuzzle me. Scooping her up and cuddling her couldn't feel any better. I down pints of water to try to stave off the hangover of staying awake all night before heading upstairs where I tear off my clothes and collapse into bed. I can't stop scratching and scratching at my legs; my skin is crawling.

I set my alarm for 5 p.m., which gives me seven hours' sleep. Go to sleep in the dark, wake up in the dark, work in the dark.

Just one more night shift to go before a break from the police station for the light relief of further training with the usual gang.

14

Abuse of Position

Autumn 2019

The secondment back to training school for a month and a half feels like coming back to the comfort of a down-lined nest. Six weeks of sheer calm and predictability, compared to the relentless churn of prisoners back on borough. This block of training doubles as a reunion with the original lot of direct entrants I started with. It's nothing short of heart-warming to be surrounded by them. Having trained the same way and having shared such a unique journey into the Met, I feel like I fit in when I'm surrounded by these siblings. We're not 'other' as we are when we're dispersed.

It's brilliant to slip back into the 'good old days' and catch up with everyone. Mostly they appear to be doing well. But our group is five down. Tom isn't here – he has failed his NIE, and is being held back in Development, tormented by his horrible sergeant who's told him in no uncertain terms he's not good enough. Nath hasn't made it back to borough either. Gabriel, Mia and Sophie have left.

The days are filled with lessons and as the course starts and finishes at the same time every day, evenings can be reclaimed as our own – no random shift pattern, overtime or uncertain finishes. We're fresh when we finish as we spend the day sitting listening rather than running around expending all our energy. This is a huge novelty.

But there is one way in which we have acclimatised to the Met: we talk shop ALL the time. Finally we have our own battle stories to share. In the space of the first lunch break in the canteen I learn that: Lexi T interviewed a fraud suspect who chain-sucked on sachet after sachet of ketchup, mayonnaise and BBQ sauce as a distraction technique (it worked); Becky from the sister class has been put in a specialist rape team, seemingly by administrative error; Lance from the sister class has charged a prolific paedophile and on raiding his home found it full of child-sized dolls.

The rumour goes round that Joel, class captain of the sister class, who has always taken the role of police officer very seriously (too seriously, some might say – he's known for wearing his stab vest to nip from his Chelsea-based police station to get his flatbread from Pret each day) stopped a train while off-duty as he smelt weed on a fellow passenger. Stopped an entire train in its tracks! He's loving the showboating, sharing his short career in vivid details, each story trying to out-extreme the last. The one that stays with me is the time he slipped on some brain matter when attending a sudden death. A woman had taken her life by jumping from a hotel to the street below, splattering on impact with the pavement below. He talked at length, if oddly matter-of-factly, about finding the chair she'd used to climb up and over the balcony railings and the spectacular panoramic view of Hyde Park that would have been the last thing she saw.

But by the end of the week, a week that for once has asked nothing more of us than that we absorb information, the masks we've been wearing that everything's great begin to slip.

We're a couple of drinks in when having laughed, joked and drunk some, Lexi T is the first to crack.

'Being a DC on borough feels like I'm a chef in a kitchen,' she blurts out. 'It's like I'm in the kitchen and I'm supposed to be making hundreds of people roast chicken; they're all sat waiting in the restaurant and they're hungry, worse, they're hangry, really hangry, but as I look around this makeshift kitchen I realise I haven't got an oven or anyone there to help me. So the orders keep flooding in, but all I can cobble together are cheese sandwiches. The orders for roast chicken keep coming thick and fast, quicker than I can get the unwanted, substandard, sandwiches out. I'm sweating, busting my balls trying and it's never enough but I'm working so goddamn hard and everyone feels let down.'

She paints this vivid, hopeless scene without drawing breath; I feel stressed just listening. Everyone is quiet for a minute, nodding. We all know exactly what she's talking about.

Then the floodgates are open and now everyone's analogies start pouring out, all variations on the theme of 'understaffed and overworked'. Processing prisoners is described as a sausage-factory production line and shelf-stacking. Trying to keep on top of the workload is plate-spinning, juggling twelve balls at once, climbing a mountain of shale the summit of which can never be reached, and being buried alive in an avalanche of paperwork and out-standing actions.

I have three of my own that I've kept to myself until this evening:

1. It's like fighting a raging fire with a small hand-held water pistol.
2. It's also like the scene in *Fantasia* where the magical broom is hit with an axe to stop it in its tracks, but each splinter becomes another broom, and soon there's an army of brooms and it's chaos. Every action I take seems to sprout five more actions, so getting work done creates more work than can ever be done.
3. I feel like a fish out of water – both metaphorically and liter-ally. I am not institutionalised and feel like an outsider. And on my worst days I spend the shift thrashing about in the system with all my might but getting nowhere, bound to perish.

Imagery aside, there is a collective feeling of shock that we're all fighting a battle that can't be won. We all agree that our working day can leave us feeling like we've been beaten up. It's hugely labour intensive for minimal results, reward or fulfilment, and we are dogged by a constant sense of failure despite our good intentions and the effort we make. The relief I feel in knowing that it is not just me who's struggling is immeasurable.

*

We're starting the second week at police HQ, when I get a text from Mel. 'Can you tell staff that I'm going to be late today?' She's sent the text after the lesson was due to start. That's odd – I'm the one who's usually late, never her. She messages me again. 'You won't believe what happened.' When we get to the break and there's still no sign of her, I call her a couple of times but still no answer.

At lunchtime she reappears with a staggering story. Being the organised soul that she is, Mel had arranged a space in shared police accommodation for this week of the course. These rooms, dished out on a first-come first-served basis, are like gold dust as those who get them are spared getting up at 4.30 a.m. each morning to hike across London to Hendon.

She moved into the digs on Sunday night and had a drink and a chat with the other two officers who'd also just moved in to their three-bedroom flat. They chatted about what they did in the Met. Mel is by far the newest. One's a very high-ranking super-intendent in the DPS (Directorate for Professional Standards, a unit that exists to weed out bent cops, think Ted's job in *Line of Duty*). The other's a sergeant who's just days away from a new role heading up a rape and sexual offences team. Before they turned in for the night, the sergeant instigated a chat to work out the following day's shower rota for the shared bathroom. Mel was second in the running order.

Today, at her allotted time, she headed to the bathroom, saying 'Morning,' to her new housemate en route.

In the shower Mel glanced around absentmindedly. Her eyes stopped at the glass pane above the door when she saw what looked like a phone pressed up against it. Then it was gone. She thought she'd imagined it. But moments later she looked back and there it was again, this time with a hand clasping it in place. She moved fast, jumping out of the shower without turning it off, wrapping a towel around herself before bursting out of the bathroom, piling into her new housemate who stumbled backwards on the landing clutching his phone to his chest.

'WERE YOU TAKING FUCKING PICTURES OF ME?' she raged.

'I've deleted it. I've deleted it!' he said, skulking backwards.

The commotion woke up the DPS superintendent and he sprang into action, calling the police, who came to arrest their house-mate for voyeurism and take him away. The officers who arrived seized the guy's phone and laptop. Another team went to his home address where he lived with his wife and baby and took all his devices as part of the investigation.

Mel was OK but in shock. Preying on a female colleague in police accommodation – it was beyond belief. Lexi T and I were horrified and sickened as she told us. There was something par-ticularly perverse and twisted about the fact that he committed a sexual offence against a colleague – a probationer colleague – when his next job was going to be protecting victims of sexual offences. He would have had access to hundreds of films of women describing their rape in a visually recorded interview. It didn't bear thinking about. And what would Mel have done if the DPS super-intendent had not been there as a witness?

That afternoon the DC in charge of the investigation comes back to Mel with an update: he has been charged. The sergeant had opted not to speak in interview, instead giving an unusually long written statement in which he denied the voyeurism offence.[1]

He stated it was all a misunderstanding. He thought he'd left his razor in the bathroom and had been using his phone as a peri-scope to peep through the window above the shower to check.

This story makes us almost as outraged as the initial crime. How is that in any way plausible! Is this guy thick as shit or what! Why not knock, one might ask (and eventually Mel's barrister does just

---

[1] Voyeurism is when a suspect observes another person doing a private act which the other person has not consented to being observed. A person commits this offence if it is for the purpose of obtaining sexual gratification.

that). It is the slack, arrogant story of someone who thought he could get away with it. This officer had stayed in police accommodation before, in exactly the same flat (once, we later found out, with a new young detective) and he knew the layout. It wasn't a moment of forgetfulness, it was intentional, planned and shockingly bold in the presence of other police.

That evening, Mel, Lexi T and I go back to the flat. The images from the phone he used have not yet been downloaded and Mel wants to know what he would have been able to see. So she stands in her clothes in the shower and directs me to hold her phone where she saw him holding it. All of her is visible from this vantage point, but there is no way to see the sink, where his razor would have been. Later these pictures are used as evidence.

*

The incident is shocking, but not the first sexual offence in the police by police a friend of mine has been victim of. She was groped by a sergeant she worked with (she also worked with his wife) at a borough party but when I say groped, he thrust his hand in her knickers and penetrated her with his fingers. She confronted him the next day but never reported it as she said it would only cause trouble. There is deeply troubling irony that assaults of this level could have taken place within the Met; the place policing other people who do these acts. Clearly these are not just freak solitary incidents but the damaging reality where there is a culture of silence and lack of proactivity to actively find, investigate and adequately deal with bad apples. Aside from low level everyday sexism which I've come to expect if not accept both in and out of work, I've come off lightly of the three of us.

I recall when I applied to the Met, telling my one friend who already worked there that I had got the job, and her response: 'Oh they'll love you.' With the emphasis on the 'you'. Her words stayed with me, disconcerting me. I didn't want to be an object at work. But now, I realise that as the months have gone on, I've made less and less effort with my appearance – no make up and dowdy clothes – hoping to blend in and avoid those looks and comments.

The Met celebrated 100 years of women in the police at the end of 2018, but women are still outnumbered more than 3 to one. Everyday sexism is as alive here as in any other workplace, sad but true. I had received those odd comments and remarks that barely land yet which all women know so well. Comments made by men oblivious to the compound impact, made in mistaken belief that we will be flattered to have our appearance or character commented on by them, that we might never have received such 'appraisal' before. I remember one day getting embroiled in an in-depth explanation of the difference between a 'fit' girl and a 'job fit' girl (office hot). In a nutshell the group explained that a 'job fit' girl is apparently someone you wouldn't look twice at or deem attractive if you saw them in regular life but, within the realm of the Met where the bar is lowered, they become attractive and shaggable.

'Don't worry,' one of the boys offered, 'you're fit fit, not just job fit.'

Another day, towards the end of a late shift, I hauled my arse up five flights of stairs to the canteen to get a chocolate bar which would be not simply a snack, but also my late lunch, my dinner and the fuel to get through the next hour of paperwork. As I walked across to the machine in the dimly lit alcove of the closed canteen, I was aware the room wasn't quite empty – there was a table of about ten guys in the far corner. Twirl purchased, I strode back to the stairs when someone from the table yelled "SCUSE ME!' at the top of their voice.

I doubled back and walked to the arch so I could see them and work out why they'd hollered at me to come back.

'Yeah?'

'Not you love. We were talking to someone who went that way,' one of them said, smirking like a schoolboy. There was no one who went the other way. It was just me and this mob up there. I turned on my heel and walked off, hearing them all sniggering behind me.

At first I was a bit taken aback. Did I just get catcalled by a gang of lads... in work? Was it so they could get a full-frontal and determine how they'd rate me out of ten? For the rest of the shift, I couldn't stop tugging my skirt down and shuddered at the sight of any male in uniform as any of them could be one of those nameless, faceless officers from upstairs who had shouted, laughed at and humiliated me.

When I got downstairs I told some of my colleagues. The women didn't say anything much, but my male colleagues waded in: 'Take it as a compliment', 'Don't overthink it', 'It's not a big deal'. But they haven't been perved at by adults since childhood. Sure, it was just bog-standard, everyday sexism. I'm used to it and have learnt to wear it as all girls and women have, but now I regret not walking over and finding out who shouted. I'm done with ignoring it, done with letting it pass. The Met is moving in the right direction, but like so many institutions remnants of the 'good old days' take a while to fully erase. All female employees are after is basic respect. Simple things, like being able to go to the abandoned canteen vending machine late at night and not be leered at by a table of ten men.

*

On arrival back at borough after the training I spot a familiar face. Karen McCaron was our SPOC (Single Point Of Contact) throughout training school; she was there to look after us, the one to go to with any problem or question. On the eve of our welcome drinks at New Scotland Yard a few weeks before our official start she was one of the key speakers and made herself known to us on several occasions throughout our initiation into the fold. I hadn't truly warmed to her – her tone was always slightly patronising – but we gave her the benefit of the doubt, believing she was one of the few people who wholeheartedly loved the pioneering, albeit controversial, Direct Entry Detective Scheme.

Now, in an odd twist of events, she has become a Detective Inspector on our borough, a promotion. When she comes to introduce herself to the Safeguarding team, for once we direct entrants know exactly who she is. Senior new arrivals in the department often give a short speech with their backstory, how many years they've worked in the police and in which departments. 'Time in' is synonymous with status, and it's gold if you can drop a few sexy specialist units in there too.

She launches in. 'Hello everybody. I'm Karen McCaron, OK. New DI. Twenty-three years' service. Probably easier to tell you the specialist units I haven't been an instrumental part of, OK! Worked on SO15 seven years. MIT five years, a LOT of prosecutions under my belt, OK. Now coming full circle back to borough for my promotion and I'll be heading Sapphire, a unit I've got years of valuable experience on, OK. Most recently I've been instrumental in delivering the Direct Entry Detective Scheme for my sins!' She raises her hands as if to say 'don't shoot me'. 'So… what can I say…' she chuckles awkwardly. 'They're my fault. Hold my hands up, I can only apologise about that, OK. So… that's me. My door's always open if you need to pick my brains about any operational challenge. I'm here for you, OK.'

I look across the room to see if I can catch Shorty or Rick's eye. I've often had the feeling that the scheme is scant of supporters, but hearing it spoken aloud by a head of department feels like a slap in the face. I'd always thought that the fact she put herself at the absolute heart of the scheme and dedicated years of her career to rolling it out meant she was a true supporter, but… I guess she was just gunning for a promotion.

Rick and I get a small kick out of making a point of reintroducing ourselves. It might be my imagination but I'm sure she walks past our section of the office double-quick ever since.

*

The training course was a welcome reminder of the breadth of the Met. It was a boost to be in Hendon brushing shoulders with officers of all different specialisms; I remembered what appealed to me during the selection process – that fact there were so many different areas you could work in, that a career in the Met is not just about climbing up the ranks but about getting experience in all different areas of policing within the Met. There are so many different departments, an officer couldn't possibly experience them all in thirty years of service. You can essentially have fifteen careers in one, which is an awesome prospect. But now I'm back, I'm starting to wonder when I'll ever get out of CSU. It's coming up to the six-month mark when I should be transferred to the Criminal Investigation Department (CID), but there's no signs of that happening.

No one seems to escape from CSU – there's just too much work and no one can leave unless there's someone to replace them. Now I see why some staff seemed to welcome direct entrants. We were their 'one in' so they could get out. Several people I know have applied and been interviewed for promotions to other teams and have been offered the post, but now await release from the borough. People wait for months, often years, to be allowed to leave. They feel trapped. One friend saw so little chance of escape that she actually resigned from the Met altogether and reapplied for a new job in another department. She had to go through the rigmarole of vetting for six months, but for her it was less painful than a never-ending period of waiting to be released from her duties here. Seems she won't be the only one... this was the last time Mel, Lexi T and I would speak as three Met detectives.

> Do we have a plan yet?

> I'm sorry to be rubbish but I've been feeling quite rough and full of cold since the weekend so am going to bail tonight. Just went to the shop practically in pyjamas as felt too feeble to get dressed – a sorry sight!

(My only contribution to the chat. This was partially true as I had adopted this 'pyjama look' almost exclusively outside work but what my friends didn't realise was that I was recovering from depression and still on the withdrawn side.)

I'm stuffed with a griefy job so unlikely to get out at any decent time anyways

No worries – I'm pretty tired as well

Another 12+ hour shift on a case I gave no shits about which is a total mess and the CPS are having a go. I mean why does ANYONE do this job?!?! I literally do not understand

It's shit

And guess what get to repeat it all again tomorrow

I can't see how it can be sustainable/enjoyable at this point

Me neither... like does everyone just cling on with the vague hope of moving to a better unit at some unidentified future point?!

Are you at the point of looking to get out?

And… why am I supposed to be excited by getting a charge when that creates an insurmountable load more of work for me to do?!

I'm just ploughing on with applications now

I hope for NFA

(No further action, i.e. no paperwork.)

And the prospect of getting torn a new one at court/getting warned for court when you are supposed to be off

Bring it. Would be way easier to stand in the box being reprimanded than actually do the work

Hahaha!

This was not done because I cannot work every second of every day, your honour

That will be my answer to everything

Justice probably won't be done because I'm too broken by the system to care, your honour

It sucks

As does getting up at 5am

Also… and definitely tmi here but… I think this job is affecting my bowel movements. Like… nobody likes to poop in a rush!

Hahaha!

I saw a junkies vag this week… First full strip search …

Delightful 😖

Like a stubbly ham sandwich

I got grabbed in custody

Unfortunate timing

Next thing I know I'm seeing a naked lady

On the upside, there's not been time to eat on my last 4 shifts, I've lost 2lbs!

Never time for food

And probably more to lose if I could just take a dump … The justice diet

(Photo of burnt black and ruined piece of toast on a chopping board)

> This is what's left of my toast whilst I got distracted doing a COPA file [case file and write up of our investigation that goes to the CPS] I feel its an appropriate reflection of how I feel

> I thought it was a doormat

> Please God tell me you didn't eat that. I've never seen such cremated toast in all my days

Lexi T is dreading her stint in CSU so much that she decides she won't do it. She quits. This doesn't surprise Mel or me. Talented as she is, she's made no secret of how she's found the job. In her exit interview she holds nothing back and lodges a complaint about their mentor, who is still crushing Tom. Following this the sergeant is moved out of the 'support' role to another department, never to be seen again.

But what will be my ticket out? I had embraced CSU, working to tackle domestic abuse before it spirals out of control, and believed I could keep people safe. Domestic abuse is far more rife than I ever realised; according to the Office for National Statistics, in the year ending March 2021 there were 1,459,663 incidents and crimes relating to domestic abuse recorded by police in England and Wales. Domestic abuse represents 18 per cent of all offences recorded by the police. And also worth adding is that domestic abuse is often a hidden crime that is mostly not reported to the police so what we do know of is the tip of the iceberg. But I hadn't anticipated the feeling of hopelessness I would feel dealing day after day with problems I can't possibly solve, of intervening to help women caught in a cycle of violence but being endlessly frustrated by the justice system.

Not all departments are like this in the Met, I know this. I'm trying to keep my eye on the future; this is just a stage, I tell myself, and try to focus where I might like to work when my probationary period is behind me. I'm most intrigued by the Murder Investigation Team (MIT) – everyone is. MIT and counter-terrorism are the most coveted places to work in the Met.

I arrange a three-day placement with MIT to shadow the team while they are on duty as the HAT (Homicide Assessment Team) for east London. I really hope I can make a good impression.

The HAT car is a response service that specialist MIT teams do on rotation; it means they are on call for live jobs. If, or rather when, someone gets murdered in east London this week, they will be called, then drive at breakneck speed on blue lights to the scene and optimise the golden hour of the investigation (the first hour after a murder is committed when all the most valuable evidence can be gathered).

The team are based in an office building hidden behind an industrial estate. When I meet the MIT team they are all really welcoming. Every single person there makes an effort to talk to me.

They tell me that when the phone goes we will rush to the murder scene, but until then it's chilled. They're happy to answer question after question after question, enjoying my fascination and enthusiasm. In a matter of hours I know this is where I want to be one day; it's such a beacon of hope to be able to see where you want to go.

The first morning I get there they are all talking about the start of Roderick Deakin-White's trial for domestic murder – a case they all worked on together. I've read about this one in the news. It's clear they all hate this guy, who bludgeoned his ex-fiancée, caving her head in with a metal bar as she showered, before fleeing, leaving her to bleed to death alone on the bathroom floor, yet who, right up until the very last minute pre-trial, stuck to the line 'she made me do it'. I find the way they worked to bring him to justice inspiring and encouraging. When someone is murdered unlimited resources are unlocked in the Met, with the result that the conviction rate for murder is over 90 per cent – the very opposite of the CSU. Every case is a team effort. While there is of course an officer in charge, they all take roles to cover every aspect of the investigation to a gold standard, so they all share the satisfaction of seeing a case brought to a successful conclusion.

That's the difference between specialist units and borough policing, a difference they explain using a jigsaw analogy. In a specialist unit you have far fewer cases, more time and resources so, if you view putting a case together like a jigsaw, you find every little piece out there to complete the full picture. Borough policing, they say, is more 'like throwing a handful of jigsaw pieces down and hoping they fit'.

We talk candidly about CSU and the Direct Entry Detective Scheme. The team tell me they think it's mad putting brand-new recruits in CSU: 'highest volume of cases and highest risk. It's the toughest place to be a detective in the whole Met!' I concede it feels like being in the trenches to their war room. They unanimously say they couldn't and wouldn't do the job I do day in day out. 'Put me in there, I'd quit the same day.' Someone else says, 'You direct entrants, have been given a hospital pass.'

'Get through and it gets better' is their mantra. The way they work, talk and treat me reassures me. Now I know that I'm in the tunnel but there's light at the end of it.

The phone doesn't ring that day. Next afternoon I bound in hoping for some action, but the shift takes a nosedive early on. A call from Warwick. I go out to the corridor to take it. Without so much as a hello he launches in, 'Where the hell are you?'

'I'm on attachment with MIT.'

Warwick has been off sick with a bad back for a month and is out of the loop. I asked permission from our inspector, who is more senior than Warwick, and his deputy, Ed, who is acting sergeant, is also well aware.

'You're what?! You have no authority to be there.'

'I asked permission from the DI. It was organised weeks ago.'

'He knows nothing about it. No one has a clue where you are. Do you have any idea how serious this is? This is unbelievable. Who do you think you are? You can't just go off on an attachment with MIT without my permission. I wouldn't have allowed it anyway. You'll come back to borough tomorrow, and that's an order.'

I'm raging at his reaction but I try to stay calm. 'I'm sorry you didn't know, but our team do. I've spoken to Ed and I asked permission from the DI as you were off before I confirmed the date with the DCI on this team. I only have one more day of the attachment left.'

'You will come back tomorrow. End of.' He hangs up.

Tears sting my eyes at being spoken over and not listened to. I put a brave face on and go back in to tell the team what happened and that I have to return tomorrow. They are indignant. 'No way! You have to stay for the final day. He sounds like a power-crazed prick who needs to get a grip. Where does he get off barking orders at you 'cause he's a rank above you when people far higher than him have approved this?'

As if he can feel his ears burning, Warwick calls back for round two. I go out to take the call, feeling sick as I click Accept. 'Hi Warwick.'

'Are you with the MIT team right now?'

'Yes.'

'Put me on to the sergeant in charge there.'

For. Fuck's. Sake. 'One moment.' I go in and say 'My DS is asking to speak to you,' making apologetic eyes at him. I hand the phone over as if it's a grenade that's about to blow.

I feel hot with humiliation as I watch the phone call play out. On a call to a man of equal rank, Warwick is clearly on the charm offensive.

'Yes, I'm out of earshot,' I hear Al, the MIT Sergeant say, shaking his head in disbelief as he stands well within earshot of the whole team. 'Well, that's not my finding from my short time with her but thanks for going out of your way to tell me.'

He hangs up. 'I'd watch your back with him. He's out to get you.'

He tells me that Warwick had said, speaking as one sergeant to another, that I had issues, was a probationer who wasn't suitable to be on attachment.

So much for my making a good impression.

But the team are supportive, and unlike CSU where my colleagues keep quiet in the face of Warwick putting me down, they rally behind me. They talk of how they suffered a tyrant boss at MIT for a time, which decimated the team as so many jumped ship. They even help me to draft an email to my Inspector to challenge his order to return to the office the next day, and the sergeant on the team writes separately, praising my conduct during my brief stint there. As much as I appreciate them being in my corner, it doesn't change his order. I go back to CSU the next day feeling mortified by the whole carry-on, worthless and totally demoralised. Shamed for taking a little initiative and having some ambition.

At 3 p.m. on what would have been my final shift with the MIT team, a schoolboy was stabbed to death in broad daylight on his way home from school in Stratford. I don't know how I would have coped with the murder of a child, I hadn't expected that.

*

> Email
> From: Warwick
> To: Jess
> Subject: JESS
>
> failed to reply to my text message

> Email
> From: Warwick
> To: Jess
> Subject: Please ignore last email – not for your information

Great, I think. He's recording everything I've 'done wrong'.

*

Our CSU Detective Inspector asks me about outstanding actions I have on some of my Crown Court cases. I confide in him that I feel I'm drowning and don't know how to complete many of these actions, having never prepared any case for a trial, let alone a Crown Court trial. I am the OIC (Officer In the Case) for anyone I charge and as such every single piece of evidence as a court document for the trial must be provided by me for both sides, prosecution and defence.

'I think we need to find you a mentor to help you learn how to tackle this,' he says. He arranges for Doug Hudson to be my mentor for the next month. This is the most brilliant news.

I already know that laughing with Doug and Oscar in the office gives me life; they both have the best infectious laughs. Their combined traits, Oscar's wit and silliness and Doug's wonderfully random episodes, brighten my days no end.

But now Doug restores my faith in the job and in myself. He explains, supports and entertains. He's a complete joy bringer. One day he claims he can do more one-legged piston squats than anyone in the office and then, unchallenged, starts doing a set in the centre of the office. It's 7 a.m. Another time he treats all the office to a listen of the song his former band recorded about celery. But in between it all, I'm learning so much from him and suddenly it all feels possible, rather than being buried by the enormity of the workload I've been tackling, often clueless and always alone.

Doug is endlessly positive and gives me motivational talks, all of them variations on the theme of 'keep ploughing on'. 'It gets easier. Every day, it gets a little easier. But you gotta do it every day – that's the hard part.'

Or, on another day: 'You're a shark, Jess.'

'Yeah right.'

'What happens to a shark if it stops swimming? It dies. So you have to keep swimming.' He's the original Ted Lasso, albeit a slightly more cruel one...

On payday Doug asks to see my payslip. I can't see why not as we are both DCs on a fixed pay scale which is directly linked to time in the job. I show him and he starts dry-retching in horror at it, staggering away from my screen bent double. 'How do you exist on that, Jess?!' he cackles and everyone in the busy office stares.

'What's his name, Snoop Dogg's, no Snoop Lion's or is it Dogg again, anyway his spliff-roller gets paid more than you!'

We're paid less than any DC ever has been as the Met has never had people in their probation (first two years of service) take on a workload like this before. So while we may have been fast-tracked into high workloads and responsibility, our pay doesn't reflect this. We're a cheap labour solution.

*

Danny Duskin's trial date is fast approaching. Yet, a month before Duskin's pre-trial review, his ex-girlfriend Ella tells me she wants to drop the case. Until I worked in the police I didn't realise that the decision to drop a case isn't for the victim to make. The prosecution can be continued victimless. However, she withdraws her support for the prosecution. I meet up with her to try and persuade her to testify. I really want her to appear in court; there are measures that can be taken so she doesn't have to face him or even be in the same room and I reassure her that we'll be there to support her on the day, that she can go for a court visit beforehand so she will be prepared, but she's resolute. Over and over she says she's sorry, until I ask her to stop. She's done nothing wrong, she just can't face him. It's been almost six months, she's likely felt conflicting emotions that whole time and doesn't want to relive what happened that day any longer; she just wants to move on with her life. I get it.

The longer I work here, the more I see that the long wait for a trial just doesn't serve victims of domestic violence and jeopardises the case itself. Six months is the minimum time it will take for a case to come to court, but that can be a year or more, months of worrying about whether they'll be believed by the jury, about the repercussions, about 'ruining' the life of someone they once loved and perhaps still do. Often it's longer, much longer. Plenty of time for the anger about the shitty treatment at the hands of their partner to fade and anxiety or guilt to set in, or for their partner to get to them even if they're behind bars.

Often the wait for the trial isn't much less agonising than the torment they live in beforehand. Victims are frequently people who've been in long, toxic relationships that have chipped away at their resolve, self-belief and worth. They imagine they won't win the case, they'll get chewed up and spat out by the courts, the partner will continue to lie through their teeth and it will fall to one word against the other. And they fear the outcome – how bad would the fallout be if it went the distance and then their partner was set free? ('You come at the king, you best not miss.') It's not that victims 'don't want to know', as is so often said by detectives when victims withdraw their support for the prosecution, it's that, as the wait goes on, these fears eat away at their belief in a case, and their ability to fight it.

Usually, the CPS throws out the case when a victim withdraws, despite still having their original statement as a key piece of evidence. This time, the CPS tries to throw out the case but I wrangle really hard to keep it, as for once, even without Ella, we still have more than enough evidence.

When I finally got the prison phone recordings I had my Eureka moment. After several hours, Ella says 'You broke my fucking nose,' and Danny replies 'I know I did, I'm sorry babe.' I play back this admission of guilt over and over and over – irrefutable digital evidence that simply doesn't exist for most domestic cases.

So Doug and I get ourselves ready to visit Danny Duskin at HMP Pentonville. I need to further arrest him for witness intimidation and interview him about the offence. I cannot imagine doing this, my first visit to prison, without Doug's help. There are so many rules and regulations to negotiate, let alone all the stuff I will need for the interview. We have to bring our own equipment and declare it, right down to the number of pens, so we 're lugging an old school recorder that looks like a slide projector to audio-record the interview. We'll have just an hour to set up and get what we need from the interview with no margin for error.

We wait with all the visitors for that day in the holding area. They're almost all women, dressed up to look their best for the visit; they seem well acquainted with each other and the system. 'WAGS,' Doug whispers to me, a tad too loudly. One woman near us is juggling an armful of baby and toddler. A guard ushers us through the area to leave our things in a locker and go through security. The corridors we walk through don't resemble a prison as depicted on TV – grey concrete walls and glass-fronted booths – but are more like a very tired primary school classroom, with little murals of puppies and flowers on the walls in an attempt to mask the daunting environment for the family. We follow our escort through the worn Victorian building, through a few doors and up a creaky staircase. At the top of the staircase he unlocks a door and without notice we walk out on to a stage looking out over the visitors' hall, where all the inmates are sitting waiting for their visitors to arrive, a sea of grey tracksuits.

Our moment centre stage is thankfully brief before we're taken down to the bowels of the building. This place is a warren. Finally we are let through a barred door into a dank and tiny room where Danny is waiting. For someone who has been incarcerated for five months already and who is about to be charged with further offences, he looks pretty chirpy.

Aware of time ticking, I try to set up the 'mobile' recording equipment but it appears to have croaked en route. This stresses me out and I try to chit-chat as the screen shows 'calibrating' for the next ten minutes. 'So, how are things in Pentonville, Danny?'

'It's a shit-hole compared to Thamesmead.'

We abandon the recorder and go for good old-fashioned hand-written. I'm confident as an interviewer by now, but this is the first time I've ever been observed. I'm not sure if it is the pressure of being watched or the pressure of being in prison that throws me off, but I choke a bit.

I start the interview shakily, and forget the caution, which I never do. I want Doug to see that all his time invested in helping me is paying off and am so frustrated at myself for making such a basic mistake. When I play Danny back the phone calls he made to Ella, where he admits to hurting her, he doesn't deny or say 'no comment' or even flinch. He says he's reformed now. I close off all possible defences he might come up with, less than confidently.

We have what we need but Doug keeps going on and on about the fact that I forgot the caution, not detecting that I'm already beating myself up about it. 'I can't believe you didn't say it. It's like the first thing you ever learn at police school. Even children know the caution. You can't just not say it in an interview. It's the law, Jess...'

'All right!' I hear myself snap and feel tears prick my eyes and start to roll down my cheeks. I can't look at him for the journey back to the police station. I hate that I let myself down in front of one of the few people who believed in me.

'C'mon Jess, you're a shark, remember. You've just got to keep swimming,' he says kindly back at the nick.

*

Josh and I are together again and I'm over the moon about it. But he has a life outside work, and weekends, and wants me to be part of it. I make it to a few events, drinks here and there, the odd dinner, but I usually attend feeling as though I've been through the wringer. Tonight we're meant to be going for dinner in Brighton with friends of his and he's begged me not to bail.

I'm on an early shift, 7 a.m. to 3 p.m.; it should be possible. But the shift runs on and it's five o'clock before I get out, and I end up dashing across town to meet him at Victoria, and burst into tears of frustration on the train. With no time to go home, I go wearing the ugly trainers, jeans and frumpy top I've been wearing all day, unmade-up and feeling incredibly fragile. Josh assures me that being around people will make me feel better. He's right, the evening is enjoyable, and a tonic, even if it is cut short by our dash to get the final train back to London so I can be in work at 7 a.m. on Sunday. Months and even years later he talks about the fact I went to dinner in my runners, it bothers him so much that I don't take care of my appearance while in the Met. I'm not sure whether it's out of concern for me or if he's embarrassed about me and how my shabby look reflects on him.

*

My month of mentorship with Doug culminates with Danny Duskin's pre-trial review. This is the final hearing before the jury

trial a few weeks later. We feel very fortunate to be at this point –
so few domestic cases go this far.

As we mill around outside the courtroom the defence barrister
approaches us and asks if we would accept a plea deal. I wasn't
expecting this! He says Danny will plead guilty to the two major
charges (which he has admitted to on the recorded prison phone
calls) if the other more minor charges are dropped. We agree
without hesitation. This is an incredible result. The guilty plea will
save the cost of a Crown Court jury trial to get to the same result: tens of thousands of pounds.

Doug and I are buzzing and we bound back to the office where
everyone gives their congratulations. Everyone except Warwick.
He's just across the room, and can hear us telling the story, but
stands out in his silence and refusal to acknowledge our success.

I contact Ella and let her know the result. She texts me later that
afternoon asking when I'm next in work as she wants to come and
say thank you and bring me flowers and a card. I think she wanted
to show appreciation that someone was in her corner and fought
her case.

*

Just before Christmas I hear a rumour on the office floor that gives
me hope: Warwick is moving on from our team. He's transferring
to a team which monitors indecent images of children. A few days
later he confirms the good news: he will be leaving in a month. He
introduces the team to Gareth, his replacement, who currently has
a black eye. He had a fight in McDonalds after the work Christmas
do and ended up with more than nuggets.

Warwick makes a point of taking me aside to tell me that this an
opportunity for me. I can make a fresh start with a new DS. It seems
an odd thing to point out having been less than unsupportive this
whole time but I take it that this is his way of burying the hatchet.

But alas, no. Hours later Warwick sends through my written appraisal. We've never had an appraisal meeting or discussion, so it
comes out of the blue.

If I had to use one word to describe what he's written about me it would be 'damning'. I stare at it in disbelief. He's kept a meticulous list of every single mistake I've made – very low level, learning the ropes mistakes – but here they have been used to evidence incompetence. Most of them are errors linked to reporting and not knowing systems or processes well. He's left out anything positive, even measurable metrics such as charges and successes at court. I've worked so hard and I'm doing just fine. I'm not expecting him to give me a round of applause but what's documented should be a fair representation.

I tell Rick and he laughs in shock. 'No wayyyyyy! I heard Warwick bragging about writing it but didn't realise it was yours. He said he'd just destroyed a direct entrant!'

Then he adds, 'I don't know why you're shocked – he's always had it in for you.'

All this time I've been registering Warwick's low-level aggression. His sneers of 'You don't know how to do...??' in mock disbelief every time I ask a question, his frosty silences and snide comments, but I wasn't aware that his daily micro-aggressions were quite so obvious to others.

I decide I'm not going to waste a jot more energy on this man, who has been against me from the start. I'm hopeful that soon I will be moved to the CID team in Hackney, which has a different approach: in CID the suspect has no relationship with the victim and is usually unknown, and the pace is slightly less hectic. Until then, I'll soon be free from this tyrant sergeant who has offered no support, only the silent treatment. He has made my time in a difficult department far more difficult than it ever had to be.

*

Josh's business is going amazingly, better than amazingly. Everybody wants a piece of it, of him, and after years of trying to make it happen he's enjoying the success. For me it feels like two different realities – the gritty, poorly paid, down-to-earth reality of the Met, and his entrepreneurial start-up, where the hours are long and the work is hard, but the money's suddenly pouring in and everybody wants to hear what he has to say. The contrast is so great that he calls the bleak stories I bring home from work 'Jessie Downers'.

'We're going on holiday, Jess. You need a break,' he says one night. He knows how much I love to travel. So I book some leave and we go, two glorious weeks in Vietnam. But the first few days I am in a state – tense, snappy, tearful, the jet lag fuelling insomnia that leaves me sobbing in the middle of the night, just trying to process everything I've bottled up for months. Months and months spent in survival mode have left me knackered, stressed, traumatised and utterly drained by the sheer volume of depressing stuff that makes up my working week. And now, in the midst of paradise, out it all comes. I suppose this is what you call decompression.

This is not at all the holiday Josh had in mind, but he tries to comfort me through my tears.

One particularly bad night I tearfully announce that I can't go on, the job is destroying me. 'So quit,' he says.

'I caaaaaaaaaan't, I'm addicted!' I wail.

He bursts out laughing. I'm sure it sounds ridiculous as I look at him earnestly through my puffy eyes. Instead this is a moment of realisation in a dark hour and (thank God) the turning point of the holiday. I also know that it's true, I am addicted – hooked on the realness of what we deal with in the Met. Real people, real lives on the frontline of an institution that exists because it's necessary that society is protected. Work that feels vital, rather than nice to have. The job, like an abusive partner, beats me up but needs me, and I stay for the tiny glimmers of hope that I will make a difference.

15

Unravelling

2020

'Morning.'

'Morning.'

'Morning!'

I'm back, ready for action. Ready to tackle the mountain of emails and salvage all the balls that have been dropped on various cases in my absence. Outside of my team, no one has noticed that I've been gone for a fortnight: all are too busy, noses to the grindstone.

'Ah, Jess!' Dan throws his arms up in celebration. Dan is the arrest guy for Safeguarding, accompanying detectives on arrests that might be tricky or dangerous.

'Morning Dan!'

'We're all ready to do your arrest enquiry when you are. Just been briefing the team.'

'Haha. Good one.'

I carry on walking and cast a glance back to see him revel in his dad joke but he's just looking at me unblinking, serious as your life. I stop. 'What? You're not serious? I haven't set that up. Today's my first day back from holiday!'

'Fucking moron! Said you knew!' He gestures to the open-plan office next door where my team sit.

'Who?'

'Warrick.'

Still, I'm unflappable today. 'Look, it's not a problem. Let me check what it's about then we can head out.'

He grins.

A quick scan through yesterday's emails reveals that I've been nominated by Warrick to go and arrest a man by ambushing him as he attends his Job Centre appointment this morning.

It's odd that I've been singled out for this mission, not least because

a) This is my first day back after two weeks off
b) Today is a spare day on the rota, free for me to catch up on paperwork. My plan was to tuck myself into a desk and wade through the post-holiday admin.
c) We arrange our own arrests. I've never known one be arranged for me.
d) This man isn't on my list of outstanding suspects. His case is nothing to do with me, and I haven't been allocated it, or informed face to face.

Something feels off about it.

I read through the files. The man is wanted for assaulting a white woman who works at the Job Centre. The fact that he called her a 'fucking white bitch' as he assaulted her and threatened to wait outside and spit at her as she left work makes this a hate crime (any criminal offence perceived by the victim or any other person to be motivated by hostility or prejudice). On further investigation he flashes as violent on our system. He has attacked female police officers in the past.

It doesn't take a genius to see that sending a white female police officer to arrest him is a red rag to a bull. I am the only white female on the team, so quite literally anyone else would have been more suitable. Like, for instance, the guy on our team who is actually responsible for the case.

Neither Warrick nor second-in-command Ed are in, so I can't ask why I've been nominated. Risk awareness is a fundamental in CSU so I know this is no oversight or mistake. It feels vindictive. Maybe Warrick is thinking of the sentencing potential if the man takes the bait and attacks a police officer. I feel like I'm being offered up to be assaulted.

Dan comes in waving a spit guard – a cover that police can put over someone's head if they spit – rarely seen in public as they look like an executioner's hood from times of old. 'Looks like you might need this.'

'Surely me arresting him is going to antagonise him?' I ask, despairingly.

'Don't worry, Jess, any funny business I'll put him on the floor. I've got a gang of new recruits coming along too.' He makes a movement as if to grab, hood and elbow-drop an imaginary man attacking me. Thank God for Dan.

In the time before we leave I grow increasingly stressed. I think about sending an email to the powers that be expressing that this is probably not going to play out well and that any resulting issue was foreseeable but I don't. There is still a put-up and shut-up culture at the Met and I think it will cause more grief than it's worth. Instead I call Josh and tell him that I'm being sent to arrest a guy for a hate crime against a white woman who happens to have also attacked police officers in the past. I feel my identity will aggravate his trigger points. It's also not lost on me that I'm being sent to arrest him at the scene of the original crime.

'Couldn't you just refuse to go? Can't they just send a guy if he hates women?' He's nervous for me.

'Well yes, I think they could but my sergeant has asserted his authority that it should be me. Anyway I just want it to be recorded somewhere that I thought this was mad and was going to end badly for me. I love you.'

Resigned to my fate of being spat at and maybe attacked, five of us drive to the Job Centre. Dan brings someone in (arrests someone) most days before breakfast and this is the first time I've seen him wear a stab vest to do it. He says he can feel that this one will be 'tasty'. It's unfortunate that today, in post-holiday elation and planning for a desk day, I put on not the plain-clothes arrest uniform of trainers, jeans and a hoodie but my polka-dot dress and heeled Chelsea.

We all wait in an empty room in the Job Centre – me, Dan and a clutch of the next batch of Direct Entrants. They're box fresh so I know how much help they'll be if something goes wrong. Feeling ill-prepared and sick with anticipation, I gabble away to the new recruits. Then we hear a voice approaching the door, 'Step this way, Mr John.'

I'm expecting him to go wild when he sees us, bouncing off the walls, leaping about the place like a caged animal and taking people down with him in a scrum, but he does nothing. Seeing that he is trapped in a room with five police officers he comes calmly. Later, when I interview him, he is polite, and minimises what happened, denying the extreme behaviour and saying he was just frustrated about his money not being paid. But the CCTV footage told a different story: even without sound it is clear he was raging, head-butting and grabbing at this woman as he screamed in her face, and needed to be removed by two security guards. I'd been lucky, the suspect had played nice, although my stress had not been for nothing.

But why had I been sent? A DS is meant to look after his team. More than any relief that I'd come off unscathed I felt more shocked at the complete absence of support and that I could be used as a pawn without any say or enough regard for my personal safety.

*

It's the end of the week, and I'm trying to wrap up a case. Over the last few days I have been speaking to a suspect via email and arranging for him to come in to be interviewed for an assault on a former girlfriend. There's every likelihood he won't but I've explained that he is circulated as 'wanted' and it's going to be much better for him to come for an interview on his terms rather than being taken from his bed on a 4 a.m. dawn raid, or arrested at the airport when he tries to jet off on holiday. I plan to interview him under caution but not to arrest him (known as a caution plus 3). The victim actively does not support any further police action, there isn't any other evidence that would be enough to go ahead with a victimless prosecution and she has now moved to Berlin so she's not at risk from him.

'We don't know the girlfriend is in Berlin,' Gareth remarks.

'She emailed me and said she is.'

'But have we got proof?'

'Her word… in writing.'

At police school we were taught the guiding principle is that you trust what the victim says. Then find out what the suspect says and go from there. You can't start questioning the victim's integrity as it undermines everything we do.

'Nick him. Why are you worried about fucking up his day?'

I go to custody and ask that they reserve a cell space for one. Luckily I've already warned the suspect that he may need to be arrested. When he arrives, we awkwardly chit-chat about the bad weather as I walk him into a corridor and tell him politely that I'm going to arrest him now. There is no etiquette book in existence that will tell you how to make conversation with someone you are about to arrest. I caution him while smiling sympathetically and uncomfortably as if to try to make it all a bit better, and then we carry on walking and talking about the rain as I lead him to custody to get the arrest authorised. I tell him that I won't put him in a cell initially, I'll do the interview straight away and then we will hopefully get him out and home as soon as possible.

Except the custody sergeant doesn't authorise the arrest – he says it's not necessary because his ex-girlfriend is overseas, so she's protected, and I can interview him as I'd originally intended. So now I have to de-arrest him, something I've never heard of happening. I feel stupid and undermined. 'Cheers for the shit advice, Gareth,' I think. I apologise to him and he seems relieved to have dodged what in his mind could have been an entire day in a cell, and ungrudgingly gives a voluntary interview.

There are just two hours of the eight-hour shift left but I've yet to have a break. I'm tired from interviewing – the sheer intensity

of the one-on-one nature of it, you can't just do them on autopilot as no two are ever exactly the same – and dehydrated. I plan
on treating myself to a coffee, juice and grilled cheese croissant
from my favourite cafe and slowly trudging through admin until
home time.

'Jess, can you nip to Leyton and do a quick interview for a guy
over there? Victim needs an interpreter and nights probably won't
be able to arrange one.'

I call to arrange the interpreter and double-check with Gareth
whether I should arrange it far enough in advance that one of the
detectives taking over from us on the night shift will be able to
head over there.

He gives me a pitying look. 'Surely you can get an interview
done for common assault in two hours?'

I mean I could if I was sitting in the interview room set up
ready to go, having teleported over there, but it's not as simple as
that, and we both know it. To conduct the interview, I will need to
get to grips with a new case from scratch. It's not a complicated
offence – man and wife married for twenty years, he slaps her, she
calls police, no previous history – but as with all domestic cases
this doesn't mean it's simple to deal with. I will need to get myself
to Leyton, and the interview, via the interpreter will inevitably take
longer. He also has a whole other team of people, some of whom
haven't dealt with a prisoner today.

I take the path of least resistance, the back-to-back prisoners.
I pack my rucksack and hurry to the Tube, hoping I won't have to
stay on too late.

I scurry through the dark, jumping puddles to try to keep my
feet less wet as the rain lashes my back.

As I come up from the Underground into the night and continuing pissing rain I realise the Leyton super-custody is more
than a walk from the Tube, so I will have to get a bus for ages to get
there. The total journey door to door from my police station takes
over an hour. By now, I'm feeling really sorry for myself. I'm weary,
tired and hungry and just want to get home before midnight but
that's looking increasingly unlikely.

I reach the (comparatively) ultra-modern and enormous custody unit, which is octagonal – it feels like an underground maze to navigate. Cells are opened contactlessly with warrant cards here rather than the old-school key I am used to. Despite being generally tech-challenged, I manage to get the live-link interpreter into the interview room. A formidable but kind Turkish woman appears on the screen and says she's ready to go when I am.

I just need to get my suspect from his cell and we're good to go. I go to the custody sergeant to let him know I'm here to interview one of his prisoners. Prisoners are signed in and out like a library book to allay the panic of an empty cell with door left ajar.

Once you get to know them or have chatted with them a bit, the custody sergeants often give away whether you're about to have your work cut out for you with a deep in-breath, raised eyebrows, muttered 'Good luck' or sometimes, in the worst cases, 'Are you OK on your own with them?' This time I get rolled eyes as if I'm in for some low-level drama.

I learn Yusuf is seventy and has been on constant watch – essentially suicide watch – since he was admitted to custody eleven hours ago. This is a key detail that Gareth didn't relay. The sergeant said he couldn't work out from the notes why he was on constant watch and that he probably didn't need to be. He must have been in distress at some point though.

At first sight my impression of the suspect is that he has the face of a loving grandfather. He looks younger than his years, is not tall but also not frail in stature. He wears smart trousers and a sleeveless white vest, the type young kids wear under their clothes. He has tanned Mediterranean skin and tufts of chest hair protruding. They must have confiscated his shirt to stop him from tying it around his neck.

I introduce myself and gesticulate that he should follow me. He looks deeply relieved to be leaving the cell. We walk to the interview agonisingly slowly as he has a limp and keeps telling me his foot is bad (he's seen the nurse, they believe it's bruised from him kicking the cell door before they left it open).

In the interview he breaks down and weeps. He apologises over and over for slapping his wife and explains how guilty he feels. It's hard to watch and at certain points I feel myself well up and have to look up at the ceiling to stop tears spilling out. After the recording stops I continue to talk to him with the help of the interpreter. He earnestly tells me being arrested today is the worst thing that has ever happened to him. He thanks me over and over for saving his life as he says he couldn't have survived much longer in the cell. He is clearly very traumatised by his time in police custody.

When I call Gareth to update him, he answers from the comfort of his own home. In my head he's reclined with his feet up, sipping on a Baileys. 'You don't mind quickly bailing him before you leave do you?' It's rhetorical.

After a long debate with the Inspector about whether this bail requested by my boss is lawful or not, I call his daughter for the final time that night to ask her to collect him and I wait with him until she arrives to make sure he's OK.

When I tell Yusuf I'm letting him go he kisses my hand. While the custody sergeant explains his bail conditions through an interpreter on the phone, my rucksack falls over and a few bits fall out. He bends down to pick up my things and right it. I am really touched by this tender gesture. A simple act of kindness that seems quite fatherly. I never expected that suspects would treat me more kindly than my boss did.

*

The day before I started in the police I sat with friends in Shoreditch House – little did I know I was sitting in the borough that would become my workplace – and they raised a toast to my new job, saying 'Go get the baddies!' We all drank to it.

When I started in the Met, very early on we had a talk from a judge who said that the suspects she had dealt with were mad, bad or sad. She said in all her years and the thousands who had been in her court she could count on one hand those that fell into the 'bad' category. So that leaves mad and sad. 'Meek' is how I would describe the majority of the suspects I interview.

When I tell friends and family that I interview alone they always exclaim, 'What if one of those wife beaters goes for you?!' There is a panic bar and a bright red button in the interview room but I've never hit it, never even come close. The furniture in the room is screwed into the floor but if someone were to lunge across the table and start smashing my head in they could do some damage before anyone got to the room.

But they don't.

When I compare the suspect's demeanour in footage from the incident, or described in statements, with that in interview, it's like a different person. It reinforces that every one of us is more than the worst thing we've ever done, and we shouldn't be defined by it. They are not wholly abusive people; they are abusive in their closest relationship(s).

Someone more cynical might say they behave well because they see me as their ticket out of custody and try to manipulate me accordingly, but the more I work with these cases, the more I see domestic abuse as a symptom that something has gone badly wrong for this person. Anger from experience, hate that's been learnt, trauma that's never been dealt with, which manifests as flares of blind rage towards the person closest to them. Abuse is a behavioural issue.

I'm not excusing what these suspects have done or the trail of destruction of all those harmed by their behaviour, but I don't think we're framing domestic abuse and violence effectively when we say 'Why doesn't she leave him' or 'I could never do that.' It's not about her or anyone else. Although, I would say to any observer that you're lucky if you find this dysfunctional behaviour unimaginable. You are lucky your own experience has not left you with the burden of unprocessed issues that emerge as abuse, because domestic abuse is rife.

The empathy I feel for suspects is one of the things that catches me most off guard about the job I do. People I work with find it amusing and take the piss. It actually makes me think very hard about the way every single one of us treats others and look at how common dehumanisation is in our society.

Laws and their enforcement hold citizens accountable for their actions. Locking someone up for domestic abuse as we currently do addresses the issue on one level – they can't abuse a partner for the short stint behind bars – but it's dealing with the symptom, not the cause. Domestic abusers need therapy, rehabilitation and support to deal with the root issues for their own benefit and for all the people they will have close relationships with in the future.

Some of the most violent domestic attacks I have encountered have been where the suspect is a juvenile (under eighteen). In one case I dealt with a juvenile suspect who gave his girlfriend the worst black eye I've ever seen. It looked like a Halloween prosthetic, it was so enormously swollen and shocking purple. He'd then told her what to say to the police after her dad called them: two versions, one that she'd walked into a pole and the other that a black man had done it. Both made up and totally failing to convince. 'A lot of people get abuse – why do you complain about it like a little bitch' was a line I remember from the torrent of abusive messages he sent her. At first his girlfriend was manipulated and hostile but later she feared he would kill her, and so she engaged with police. By then she had found out she was pregnant with his baby and he had threatened to come round and cut the baby out, among other threats to kill.

It was deeply troubling behaviour. He pleaded guilty to multiple charges relating to his ex-girlfriend at youth court – a good outcome in theory but as far as I can tell nothing really happened, no meaningful sentence. He was still a risk to his ex, and a risk waiting to happen for subsequent girlfriends.

As it stands, we forgive those who are young but often miss an opportunity to help and intervene in a meaningful way at this early stage. Those who commit the most extreme and 'mad' offences need help and get it in secure hospitals, but what about everyone else, the majority, who get lost in the fog and quagmire of the grey area in the middle? Domestic abuse is a repeated behaviour. The average perpetrator of serious domestic abuse needs rehabilitation, albeit less than those suffering from the most severe mental disorders. And yet our only response is to lock them away as if they are beyond help, and when they are released, leave them to start the pattern again. The longer I work here the more I am convinced on all fronts, emotionally, societally, financially that therapy and rehabilitation is what's needed to win the war on domestic abuse, not simply incarceration.

But I keep this opinion to myself at work as I'm already called a bleeding heart for the sympathy I feel for everyone's plight.

*

We're dropping like flies now, our class of direct entrants. Georgia and Jake resign, but its Mel's resignation that hits me in the gut. It feels like the end of an era. She's becoming a fire-fighter and tells me the shifts and work–life balance at the London Fire Brigade are in a different league. She sends a goodbye email to her borough which starts 'As a Direct-Entry detective, I daresay we deliberately weren't told much about the role prior to joining because of the dire reality of what it is at the moment.' She acknowledges the impact of the job and that her colleagues 'martyr themselves' to do what they do.

I wake up one afternoon, marooned in the middle of a set of night shifts, and lie in bed thinking I've lost all my friends. I know this hadn't happened overnight, but lying there I feel panic-stricken that my social life has completely fallen away. I really feel the loss. Last night a colleague asked me if friends and family had noticed a change in me since joining the Met. He meant the evolution that officers go through to grow a thicker skin and detach from the horrors of everyday working life. I don't know the answer; the only change they'll have noticed is that I've disappeared.

I decide to get out of the house and head to get my hair cut as what was once long, beachy hair has degenerated into a scraggy mane, which will happen if hair is uncut for a year. I'm wearing a hoodie, leggings and my 'dog walking' jacket (I have no dog). A layer of moisturiser was all I could muster before embarking on this trip. I've always had my hair cut in a walk-in £10 barber's shop in Islington. The set-up is no frills, the hairdressers are quick and cut so much hair that they're more experienced than hairdressers you'd pay eight times the money for. No restlessness, dry chit-chat, bouffant blow dry or limp waves that always look weird and never hold at the end. My hairdresser today asks how much I want taken off and goes about it. She discovers the drugs-test tuft, which I try to explain. Continuing without another word, we're almost done, until a tide of grief seems to spill out of her in a wail. 'Such a shame!' she laments, running her fingers through my hair. 'So many greys for someone so young.' She shakes her head in sorrow while stroking the crown of my head. I ignore the sentiment and clutch the hidden compliment of 'so young' in there. I don't ask her how old she thinks I am but tell myself she's probably misjudged it by a decade or two, misguided by my 'pre-pubescent child before they discover fashion' outfit.

It's true that I've gone from not having a single grey hair to having quite the crop of pure white ones. At first I used to pluck the odd one out, put it against something dark and marvel at it, but there are far too many to keep that up. I went home and read that stress has been scientifically linked to greying. I even think I felt it happening on some days when I would get a headache and tingling around the hairline that felt like someone was constricting a belt around my head. Although it's cosmetic I find it moment-arily worrying to think what else the stress is doing to my body. Beyond the loss of pigment from my hair, the total breakdown in my work–life balance is what feels momentous. Burnout isn't limited to the work, no aspect of my life escapes; mentally, physic-ally, socially, romantically everything feels shot.

I'm with Josh, which I had longed for more than anything, and we're living together. On the face of it everything looks prom-ising. I know this is a precious final chance for us but I'm at cap-acity trying to keep my head above water. My struggle at work is dragging him and the relationship down with me. It puts me in mind of those tragic stories where someone swims out alone to save a person in some murky lake or raging river and neither survive.

*

I look at the case file that has been slapped on my desk with a cere-
monious 'going nowhere' and I've never seen the offence this man
has been arrested for before: 'violence for the purpose of securing
entry into a premises'. I'm curious about this obscure offence and
read the legislation as I start to review all the evidence. I read the
officer's arrest statements, the transcript from the 999 call and
watch the body-worn video from the arrest. Jon is twenty-seven
years old, he's black and I have this quite sickening gut feeling that
this would have gone a different way if he wasn't. If either of my
brothers, young white guys, had banged on the door to their home
to gain entry, would they have been arrested? I doubt it.

I go to interview him and learn he's opted to not have a solicitor. The custody sergeant laughs. 'In all my years I've never seen
anyone arrested for that. What a non-offence!' I check and double-
check with the suspect that he doesn't want even an initial chat
with a legal representative – they're free and independent. He says
it's a big misunderstanding and he just wants to explain it all to
me and he does just that. It all tallies with the evidence I've seen.

I present my findings to Gareth, to decide the outcome from
my investigation, knowing there is only one way it can go – immediate release, No Further Action. 'A neighbour called the police
from the block of flats because Jon was banging on his own front
door to be let in at 2 a.m. He had his girlfriend staying over; she
doesn't live there. They fell out over something, he went outside
for a cigarette and she locked him out from his own flat from
within. He tried to call her and get her to let him back in until
his phone died and at that point he got quite desperate, having
nowhere he could go, no one to call and nowhere to sleep, so he
banged away on the door.'

I can't help but add, 'He should never have been arrested as he
hasn't even committed this odd offence. I looked at the legislation
and being a displaced residential owner is a defence. He has no
previous domestic history. Essentially he was just trying to get back
into his own house. He calmly told the officers that and showed
them proof of address so I don't get why he was arrested. As you
said it's going nowhere, so can I go and let him out?'

'No, we'll get him charged.'

'What?!'

'He's admitted it.'

'Admitted what? That he was locked out? You can't charge him for that, it's not fair. He hasn't done anything wrong and he has a defence in law.'

'Well, he can tell that to the court, can't he? Request he's remanded too, to make sure he shows up to his hearing.'

I'm raging but trying to stay calm. This is lunacy. I feel compromised enough having to put the file together for the CPS to charge him, but putting in an application to keep him in the cell overnight I simply can't do. It's wrong to deprive someone of their liberty for no reason, it's a violation of a basic human right. I go and speak to the custody sergeant.

'I've been told to appeal for him to be remanded by my sergeant but I just don't agree. What do I do?'

'Well, you have to do what he tells you, but I'd just do it badly and it won't go through, will it?'

Hours later I am well into overtime and finally charging this young guy. He's gracious towards me, which makes the ordeal worse. I'm sickened that I've played a part in this. I can see that at best his naivety in not using a solicitor has been exploited to get a charge.

The piss-poor application for remand, with no reasons cited for keeping him in custody overnight, is thankfully unsuccessful and as I show him out of the front of the police station, I tell him to look up the legislation as he has a clear defence. I've read up on it and I think it's important he knows. It's well outside my professional remit but it's a statement of fact.

The next day a reviewing CPS lawyer contacts me about the case as he doesn't believe the charge should stand, owing to the defence in law. He throws the case out and the charge is dropped. I thank him over and over again but remain deeply disturbed by this, to my mind, racist incident.

*

Like everyone, we watch lockdown 2020 inching towards us with a sense of disbelief. Surely Covid-19 will not come here; surely it will stay, like SARs, on the other side of the world? Then as other European countries lock down and it starts to feel like we are dragging our heels, the country is told to go home and stay there. Except that when you work in Safeguarding in an inner-city borough, lockdown is very far from the sourdough-perfecting, garden-tending idyll some of my friends are experiencing. As a frontline service it is business as normal for us, not least because the relentless confinement of lockdown has brought a fresh, inescapable hell to those living with abuse. Domestic-violence charities are reporting an enormous spike in cases of abuse. As Josh puts it, 'locking down with an abuser is like being put in a swimming pool with a Great White shark.'

Interestingly, in CSU, this raised number of reports does not result in an increase in domestic abuse prisoners, although we are more stretched as there are fewer staff present to deal with them (a significant tranche of the workforce is shielding at home). The pandemic at last seems to have forced response officers only to arrest when absolutely necessary, filtering out some of the arbitrary arrests that might have once been made in the name of positive action arse covering. Those who darken our doorstep during the pandemic are legitimately here.

Down in custody, early Covid measures (pre-lateral flow days) extend to asking suspects with Covid symptoms to wash their hands on arrival. Then they are led, custody officers stomping ahead of them down the corridor shouting 'GET BACK! COVID COMING THROUGH! STAY BACK!' – as if this person could blow at any minute and we're in the blast radius – to a cell in a row now called the 'Hot Zone' where they are given a face mask (the other corridor of cells is now the 'Cold Zone'). On the little whiteboard affixed to all cell doors, rather than 'spits' or other useful info about the person within, *Covid-19* is written. This is somewhat more tactful than the hospital where my brother works, where they refer to non-Covid and Covid patient areas as 'clean' and 'dirty' parts of the hospital. (In custody the on-call doctors will not go near someone who says they have Covid-19 symptoms.)

Legal representatives are not attending police stations during the pandemic so phone calls and video calls are set up for residents of the Cold Zone. For Hot Zone prisoners we throw them a burner phone (not a smartphone) in a plastic evidence bag to have a call with the solicitor.

To conduct the interview we don a pair of blue latex gloves, a plastic apron and a single-use face mask, stand on the threshold of the cell and shout questions to our prisoner. We tell him to sit on the bench, which is two metres from the door. Occasionally he can't hear what we say and instinctively gets up to close the gap. 'No, no, no, no! Sit down, stay there, we'll shout louder!' we cry, retreating into the corridor. Instead of recording an interview, which would need both suspect and DC to be close enough to the mic, we have to write contemporaneous notes of every word as it's said. As a left-hander, writing has always been a drag for me. My claw-like pen grip is awkward and my ink-smudged little finger smears even the most quick-drying ink. I've never been more relieved to have a 'no comment' interview.

Then, with relief we vacate the cordoned markings off Hot Zone via the Cold Zone, we bin the gloves, apron and mask, hand-wash to the Peppa Pig song, then head back upstairs to hot-desk as normal in close, maskless proximity to our colleagues. Only the DIY buzz-cuts give away that the world is changed here.

When I get home to Josh I have to decontaminate on the landing of the attic flat. Stripping off, the ball of discarded clothes tossed in the washing machine drum before jumping in a scalding hot shower. My homecoming ritual.

*

It's the weekend, not that we can go anywhere or see anyone (though this suits me fine: I'm so perpetually tired, *Gogglebox* is my idea of a social event). I arrive in work having enjoyed my peaceful commute in a private Tube carriage and a walk through the deserted streets of London. Checking my emails, Sana's name flashes up, one of my victims. Her ex-husband Rashid has broken his bail conditions – and lockdown – to harass and stalk her yet again. Every week there is something. She is tormented by him and just can't be free.

Rashid is the thorn in my side. Three times now I have arrested him, once in the supermarket where he works, five minutes from Sana's flat – and three times the court has released him on bail prior to his court case. But Sana is getting desperate. Rashid was brought in after he broke into her flat at night, while their children were in bed, forcing his way in through her bathroom window (he was witnessed climbing the drain-pipe to get to her third-floor flat) where he attacked her and stole her phone. Neighbours heard her screams and the children shouting 'Don't hurt mummy', and thankfully intervened. He is charged with burglary and assault. Looking at the files of their history, even before this incident there was a charge for ABH against him and a domestic rape allegation on file, and many other details which paint the painful picture of an in-escapable abusive relationship.

Sana is really scared of him and it's not surprising, considering the original crime, that she can't sleep soundly in her bed at night. While she waits for the court case to happen Rashid is growing bolder and bolder, and no one is effectively stopping him from stalking her. I've tried my best to help her, I arrest him and drive him to court myself, but each time we put in an appli-cation for remand (to lock him up before his trial), he seems to wriggle out of it. The one time he was remanded he appealed and was let out permanently for a family wedding. The court doesn't seem to take the threat he poses seriously despite the finding that stalking behaviour has been identified in nine in ten murders, and in half of all stalking cases the ex-partner is the perpetrator. In fact, if anything, the system is making it worse – annoying him and leaving him complacent that whatever intervention takes place he'll always walk free. Yet another domestic-violence trial that is too long for the victim's safety and peace of mind. And lockdown means his trial will be put back even further.

*

I get a WhatsApp message from Mel to say she's back with the
police.

'You came back?'

'It's just a cameo! So... rather grim... am being drafted in for
Body Bagging duties as of this week.

"New initiative by LFB (London Fire Brigade) and MPS
(Metropolitan Police Service) to support the NHS".'

Mel is part of a PMART (Pandemic Multi Agency Response
Team), which uses vehicles containing a medic, DC, PC and fire-
fighter who will deal with the 25 per cent of fatalities that are
predicted to take place at home. The team will come in wearing
full protective gear, the DC to check the body for signs of foul play,
the medical professional to certify the death, a PC and a firefighter
to bag and move the body in a 'dignified manner' and take it away.
I picture the bodies placed in mass graves like times of old when
London was struck by the bubonic plague. It doesn't seem real.

Interestingly, following her briefing, Mel says that the Met
have mostly sourced the police element from the Directorate of
Professional Standards. It seems an unlikely choice – the DPS are
very desk-based and deal with internal police complaints and
disciplinaries – but the logic must be that those in charge of integrity and professionalism will handle these extremely sensitive
transitions with due care.

I speak to Mel at the start of week four of what quickly feels like
an infinite lockdown to find out how it's going. I ask what she's up
to, relentlessly, every single shift.

'It's pretty straightforward to be honest, if grim. Once you've
seen a few dead 'uns you've seen them all.'

'How many daily?'

'Somewhere between twenty and fifty per day across the whole
of London. Our car deals with between one to three cases per
eight-hour shift as each one takes about three hours with travel
time, admin etc.'

'Where on earth do you take them all?'

'That's the worst bit... we don't! We wrap them up, then
LEAVE the body in the house for funeral directors to collect. In

an ideal world the funeral director would arrive while we're still on the scene, but they've been so backed up that hasn't happened much. Longest I've heard a body being wrapped and left awaiting collection: twelve hours. I'm not going to lie, the worst bit is putting a plastic bag over their head and then we wrap them up in a sheet of black bin-bag and gaffer-tape it all together,' she says matter-of-factly.

This pandemic is so different for everyone. Sana, locked in her third-floor flat trying to homeschool tiny children who are climbing the walls, while Rashid lurks menacingly in the park her home overlooks. My parents saying they've never seen such a beautiful spring. Josh and I starting each day doing a floor workout to power ballads or the *Rocky* soundtrack in our attic flat, which suddenly feels a whole lot smaller. He spends all day at home on Zoom. Mel criss-crosses the city, body-bagging. And the streets of London are empty but for the foxes and a swirling vortex of manky pigeons reclaiming Elephant and Castle roundabout.

*

'Jess, could we nip upstairs for a chat?'

I'm surprised at this overture from Gareth. I've worked under him for months now, but it feels more like a couple of weeks. In fact, what with a run of nights, then lockdown, which seems to distort the passing of time, I've not seen all that much of him.

He takes me upstairs to the canteen to have 'the chat'. He tells me that I won't be able to move across to CID for the foreseeable as I am 'sub-standard'.

I'm shocked.

'In what way am I "sub-standard"?' I ask. So much for my fresh start. He ruffles some papers in front of him but doesn't answer. 'What am I doing wrong?'

'We'll have a Regulation 13 meeting and can discuss that in the meeting.'

'I don't agree that I'm sub-standard.'

'You can put that forward in the meeting.'

'What does Regulation 13 mean?'

'It's a meeting about your performance.'

I assume he means the progress I'm making, like an appraisal, but when I get back to my desk I see that the email invite to this meeting has a couple of documents attached: Warwick's comedically damning appraisal and, a new revelation, the list of every small mistake I've ever made, started by Warwick and continued diligently, fervently even, by Gareth. There are about twenty items, including 'mistakes' such as failure to obtain authorisation to attend a Met carol concert, a delay in providing interview transcript to CPS in case 01/78723/20 (one of maybe forty documents for this case, my first ever at Crown Court, which had resulted in conviction), but nothing that resulted in anything actually going wrong or caused complaint. Seven of the twenty things happened in the first two weeks I was working with Gareth when we hadn't actually met. And what about the things that have gone right? Is there a parallel list somewhere with all my successes, which would far outweigh mistakes? It feels very deliberately skewed. Is it common practice in the Met to keep a list like this for probationers? To keep a list of an individual's mistakes, not to help them improve but to make a case for them being sub-standard?

I ask Birdy if he has time to nip round the back for a coffee, and pour the whole horrible story out to him. Birdy, as well as being a friend, is also a Federation rep, the police union. Birdy's not impressed by my story, not at all.

'And he never told you the purpose of the meeting he's arranged, the snake?'

'No, he said it was about my performance.'

'He's trying to fire you, darlin'.'

'What?'

'Regulation 13 — Discharge of probationer. A chief officer can dispense with the services of a probationer if he considers that the probationer is physically or mentally not fitted to perform police duties, or that the probationer is not likely to become an efficient or well-conducted constable.'

'You're kidding me.'

'Don't worry, he's got no grounds for this. It's meant to be used when all other support options are exhausted. You're a young officer doing your best and learning. From what you've shown and told me he's given you no support and there's nothing wrong with your performance. Seems like a shit-covered baton-handover job, if you ask me. Warwick has made his assessment and Gareth's run with it hell for leather. Probably wants to use you as a case study for his workbook. Looks good if they remove the dead wood – but you're not it. Don't worry, darlin', we'll take him on and we'll win.'

At first I feel outrage: you could get rid of every single probationer on this basis. Then I feel broken by the unfair treatment, as if all my hard work's been for nothing. And then something inside me sparks up. Nothing fans the fire in my belly like injustice. I might be being forced out but I won't go quietly without a fight.

I meticulously prepare for the Regulation 13 as if it's a suspect interview or exam, reading up about poor management and abuse of process. This leads me to workplace bullying. To my mind bullying is something that happens in the school playground, not the office, but as I read down the list of behaviours and examples, I realise almost every box is ticked. Considering I work with abusive characters day in day out, it has taken a while for the penny to drop and to see that Warwick's and then Gareth's microaggressions, undermining and criticism amount to workplace bullying. But why me? It's anyone's guess; perhaps because I was 'other' as a Direct Entry detective, female, perceived to be vulnerable or insubordinate... Maybe it was good for Gareth's workbook to be seen to fire someone who was 'sub-standard'. The truth is I'll never know, and whichever motive triggered it, there is no reasonable excuse for bullying behaviour in any circumstances. Same as any other abuse.

I read and I read for hours and hours, wanting to understand. I find a cross-organisational study showing that 70 per cent of employees have either been bullied or witnessed bullying in their workplace. If a victim has been employed less than two years, the

victim has no legal recourse. This legal loophole seems all too familiar to me.

I feel a surge of relief as I read the official Met Policy: 'All bullying
is unacceptable and should not be tolerated'. I don't have to put up
with this a day longer.

Figuring that, if I don't speak up, the only side of the story
anyone will have is Warwick and Gareth's, and yet feeling like I'm
committing career suicide, I contact the borough Superintendent
and then, going right to the top, the borough Commander to ask for
a meeting. Amazingly, they both agree. The borough Superintendent
asks to see a sample of my alleged 'sub-standard' work and says it
is impressive. The borough Commander, not normally in touch
with a lowly probationer, grants me a meeting and listens carefully and assures me that bullying sickens him. I write a document
outlining and evidencing the treatment, which is difficult as it's
such an insidious behaviour. I sum up my experience of working
under Warwick and Gareth, finally admitting that working for them
makes me feel 'hopeless, undervalued, undermined, humiliated and
demoralised'. The thought that my side of the story is being heard
makes me feel as if the cavalry have arrived in the nick of time, just
as I was about to go into battle alone, unarmed and on foot.

On the day of the official Regulation 13 meeting I have Birdy,
wearing his Federation hat, to represent me. I'm bricking it but
having someone like Birdy in my corner is deeply reassuring. Once
the introductions to the member of HR and minute-taker are done,
I watch in disbelief as he tears Gareth a new one, pointing out how
out of line and unfair this whole fiasco has been.

'Look, we can carry on with this joke of a meeting,' he tells
Gareth and the woman from HR, 'but if we do, it's all going to be
recorded and revealed, what you and Warwick have been doing to
this young DC.'

Gareth is red and lost for words, the meeting is quickly
abandoned and the allegations are permanently struck out, more
or less before they started.

*

So what happens now? I have only thought as far as this battle. I presume I'm free of the bullying, and grateful, so bloody grateful to Birdy. If he hadn't looked out for me I would have walked in and been buried in that meeting without realising what it was even about.

I receive an email twenty minutes later from Gareth asking where I am and telling me to come back to 'the room where it happened' to meet with him one on one.

'I can't still be on his team after that showdown, it's only going to get worse!' I remark to Birdy. 'I'm not going.'

'You have to go, he's still your sergeant.'

Back I go, and blurt out 'Are you going to apologise?' as I walk in and face him.

'No,' he replies bluntly.

*

What felt briefly like victory pales into insignificance. I feel like I have won the battle but lost the war.

There is no process in place to deal with the bullying; it feels as if I'm the first person to raise it. It seems to me that workplace bullying is really common but largely suffered in silence and unreported, or at least un-actioned.

After refusing to work with Gareth I'm offered a move onto another team, but still in CSU, in the same office as the two men who've abused their positions and made my life miserable. I don't want to work with or near them or ever see either of them again. This is possible in an organisation as huge as the Met where everyone of the same position and rank does the same role, but no one makes it happen for me, despite my pleas.

I'm asked to repeat my allegations of bullying over and over to various people, from the Detective Chief Inspector originally charged with the investigation to the faceless DPS (Directorate of Professional Standards) reporting portal and many of my colleagues. I am asked what I want to happen. I say, 'I hope that this will be thoroughly investigated and dealt with. I also hope a better system is put in place to protect officers in their probation from not being supported and unduly managed out (particularly

Direct Entry detectives). I wish to continue working in the Met. I hope that I am granted a rotation and can leave this toxic experience far behind, from this day forward, as I focus on learning and progressing in a supportive environment.'

I can't believe there isn't a standard investigation process; we have one for quite literally everything else. They say my bullying claims will be looked into but they don't say how, or give me a timeline. But for all the lip service, to this day there is no official record of my allegations and no investigation was done. Nothing happened.

The message this sends is 'what you say happened to you is of no concern to us'. That's how I receive it and I understand better than ever before how countless women feel when their rape and domestic abuse cases are dropped, as the majority are, by the CPS.

I'm struggling in the aftermath of all the drama. The impact over time and the final fight took all the strength I could muster. I'm exhausted. I fought my corner but now I have nothing left. The bullying and its lack of resolution is the final straw. I'm signed off, burnt-out and stressed, apparently also suffering from PTSD.

When I ring Occupational Health, the nurse says she can't find my psychological assessment on the file.

'What do you mean?' I say.

'Well, to work in CSU, because it's a really high trauma area of policing, you have to first be assessed.'

She won't hear it that new recruits have been put in there, although this is exactly what happened. None of us Direct Entrants ever received a psychological sign-off to work in this area.

Should I stay and keep going or quit this mad, all-consuming role that has taken its toll on every aspect of my life? I spend a short convalescence in the London sun, going back and forth in my mind. Yet I've worked so hard to get to this point, I am crippled with indecision. I'm frazzled, my thought processes like a knotted-up ball of wool as I try to make sense of it all.

Josh wants me to leave – he says he can hardly bear to see the way this job is shredding me up. In the aftermath he often finds me sitting on the floor in the lounge with my back against the sofa sobbing. He comes and sits beside me and holds me. I worry that there's only so many times he can scrape me off the floor before he starts feeling like my carer... maybe it's too late and he already does.

I so wanted it to be different. The disconnect between how I thought the role would be and the reality was undeniable. Day after day, I drown in the misery that one human can inflict upon another. It feels too hard to shoulder the trauma that comes with the job when I know there is so little chance I can help with the justice system as it stands. The thought that springs to mind time and time again is that I'm sick of looking at people doing shitty things to each other and feeling powerless to help despite my best efforts. Although I'm torn, on balance I'm being harmed more than I help in this role.

I realise that is not sustainable, I can't do it to myself any more, and so, with a heavy heart, I resign.

For one last time I walk through the doors of the police station to hand in all my trappings of being a police officer: warrant card and weapons, Met vest and MPS Oyster card. I don't know why the usual protocol of an exit interview isn't extended to me. Maybe it's felt I've said more than enough already.

It was the most difficult choice to walk away. I had such hope in this opportunity, and I had invested so much in this new career – I had felt part of something. Giving up felt like losing a job, a home, a family, a purpose and an identity all in one. I felt so sad that it had come to this.

For the last few years everyone I knew, and everyone I didn't, had asked me avidly about my job, then squirmed at the grim stories they wanted to hear. Without fail everyone would say 'I couldn't do that' while barely knowing the half of it. My Direct Entry friends react with little surprise. Ten of us have left now.

This is a human story about human cost and in the end that cost was too high.

Lexi T texts me: 'Welcome back to normal life.'

16

On Reflection

I was brought into the Met to patch a problem. Having lived and breathed it, I find myself wondering if I failed the Met or the Met failed me. But I conclude: neither.

Working as a frontline police officer, or indeed in any frontline blue-light role, is not simply a job but rather an all-consuming life choice. A survival exercise where few come off unscathed. This is a job where bad news is our bread and butter. The job of a detective, to investigate serious and complex crime, only exists because of the terrible things people do to each other. The fact that our intervention or lack of action could result in someone's harm or death is surely one of the heaviest responsibilities a job can demand. Every day police detectives encounter more injustice, suffering and trauma than the average person would in a year. Every single day. The cumulative effect of this is massive.

I knew this on a rational level when I joined – in my naivety, the prospect of dealing with cases of life-and-death importance was part of the appeal – but the emotional reality that came with that exposure, day in day out, was something I couldn't prepare for. The longer I worked in Safeguarding the more I realised the job posed an impossible dilemma. If you care too much, you get hurt by your work. If you harden and become detached, caring less, then you lose the compassion that drove you to do the job in the first place.

In joining the Met I had thought only about what I had to give and of the impact I hoped to make. I never considered what I would have to take and the impact of that. The uncomfortable reality is that key workers on the frontline are often harmed by the traumatic incidents and the hostile working conditions they find themselves exposed to. A study by the charity Police Care found that one in five UK police officers suffer with PTSD, post-traumatic stress disorder, from our involvement in the work we do, from what is seen and experienced, and from the impact of the conditions and systems within which we operate. A police officer dies by suicide in the UK every two weeks.

The exposure and burden of responsibility of the role has been intensified by the UK government's austerity cuts to public services since 2010. Fewer people to do the job results in more for each worker to do – far, far more than can ever be done. The backlog of cases, unnecessary arrests and insufficient rehabilitation of offenders all add to the stress. Top this off with the fact that shift workers are more likely than workers on regular hours to report poor mental and physical health and social wellbeing, and it is little wonder that police detectives are left, like so many frontline workers, feeling ineffective and overwhelmed.

I joined this public service with the belief that I could make a difference. But in CSU, the department I was working in for domestic abuse and rape, the justice pathway renders the majority of our investigations futile. On a daily basis it felt like the Met's mission – to keep London safe and achieve the best outcome in the pursuit of justice and in support of the victim – was frustrated by the CPS's success-driven objective to take forward only those cases with a realistic prospect of conviction, i.e. cases they're more likely to win.

The police fully investigate every single report of domestic abuse and rape and in 90 per cent of all cases the suspect is known. And yet the vast majority of cases are blocked from being charged by the CPS. The CPS's charging code is not fit for purpose for domestic abuse and rape, which are predominantly crimes against women. The nature of these crimes does not fit the system in place to access justice, which is why prosecution rates are woefully low. The CPS don't take into consideration the fact that there can be no realistic prospect of conviction, as by their very nature these crimes usually take place behind closed doors and the evidence is mostly one person's word against another. The evidence they require to meet the threshold to charge can't be met by these crimes against women, so they are excluded. The standards are discriminatory. Most female police officers I know wouldn't report it if they were raped. Denying justice to these women is unjust and nothing short of systemic misogyny. The fault in the justice system lies with the CPS, yet it is the police who constantly get bashed in the media for a lack of prosecutions. Above anything else I encountered during my time in the Met, this issue with the CPS made me feel the most enraged and hopeless as a detective and a woman.

Everything I saw of jury trials made me believe in the courts as a route to justice. But even those cases that do get tried take too long to come to court, further traumatising the victim. The legal adage 'Justice delayed is justice denied' is surely true here.

Tip into this mix the Direct Entrant, an awkward entity, a probationer expected to shoulder full duties and responsibilities while learning on the job, willing and able but wholly inexperienced. Never before have the Met had officers take on this level of workload at the very lowest end of the pay scale. Personally, I was up for that challenge as I took the long view and saw the Met as a career. I do, however, seriously question whether it's responsible to put brand-new recruits in Safeguarding units, the most overburdened area, known to carry the highest risk and volume of crimes, with significant exposure to trauma. We were thrown in and whatever became of us was collateral damage. Plugging the hole in borough detective numbers was the objective, the wellbeing of the lab rats in the experiment a side issue. Internal prejudice made life harder. While most embraced our arrival (as you would be grateful for help on a sinking ship), I was certainly not the only Direct Entrant to work alongside colleagues who viewed us as something 'other' that undermined the established order of things.

We are asking too much of frontline officers and blue-light workers. They are not infallible saviours, not superhuman, but ordinary people, like you or me – people who need support to do a job that is ceaselessly demanding, a job that often harms them in the process of trying to help others.

17

Result

It takes me a while to adapt back to my newly reclaimed life. Pangs of loss flare up when I least expect them. Usually at night, in the quiet on a Tube escalator when I'm reminded of travelling in for a night shift. For a moment I feel panicked at the thought of never being part of that world again. I know I'll never be able to fully let it go – the adrenalin, the human stories, the drive to right a wrong.

*

In June Mel and I head to Southwark Crown Court, more than two years after she was watched in the shower by a sergeant while staying at police accommodation.

I think of the very first court case I witnessed with Helen before I joined the Met, and of heading to Snaresbrook Crown Court with some of my cases; I had thought I would be in court every other week, despatching my cases towards justice. It seems odd that one of the crown court cases I have been most involved with is my friend's, a friend who was recruited to the Met exactly the same day as me, and that the defendant is another officer, albeit senior ranking.

This case has always felt incredibly important, not simply be-cause it's personal, but also because of his potential to cause harm as a detective sergeant who, the day after committing a sexual offence, was due to take up a post leading a rape investigation team, where he would have access to countless victims and files and files of visually recorded interviews with women going into detail about their rapes. That's a horribly inappropriate role for anyone who objectifies women.

The trial's significance is amplified by the shared heartbreak and rage we all feel about the horrific offences Wayne Couzens committed by abusing his power and position. I was in the same year at the same university as Sarah Everard. But you didn't have to know Sarah to feel deeply affected by her kidnap, rape and murder; her plight has been every woman's worst nightmare since childhood. (At the time of Mel's trial he is yet to plead guilty.)

Mel has waited so long for this day. I accompany her every day of the four-day trial. In the two and a half years it's taken to get to trial she's left the Met, but she is yet to have closure. All the while he has been suspended on full pay.

Before the trial we ask the OIC (Officer in Charge), a detective from the DPS (Directorate of Professional Standards – the unit fictionalised AC12 is based on), what will happen to the money he's received if he's found guilty. She winces, 'Nothing – I know it doesn't seem right but there's no law to take it back.'

On Day 1 of the trial Mel gives her evidence from behind a grubby curtain in the courtroom so that he can't watch her (although we see him in the hallway, where he is able to come and go as he pleases). Mel's new employers, the Fire Service, send along a mentor to sit in the courtroom as a gesture of support. I sit alongside and feel so anxious for my friend. It's intimidating, giving evidence in front of twelve people who are there to determine whether they believe your account, and withstanding a barrister picking holes in what you've said, but Mel does well – slow and steady. At certain points during cross-examination she becomes tearful, her voice catching slightly as she answers the defence barrister's questions. Her reaction catches me off guard and makes me emotional. Mel is one of the strongest people I know, and what happened to her has become such a well-worn story I sometimes forget the impact on her in my outrage at the crime itself. That afternoon the senior ranking police officer gives his evidence as a witness.

On Day 2 of the trial the defendant gives his evidence. I sit listening to the sergeant explaining to the jury that he was using the phone as an extension of his eyes to get visuals on that precious razor, indignant at the gall of him. He starts off by making out that he's a paragon of exemplary policing – super-efficient, good degree, speaks languages. Yet there's also some nonsense about him being dyspraxic, although I think he meant to say autistic – he was so completely fixated on his razor that he didn't think of the naked woman behind the door, just two metres away, despite his knowing she was in there. He is neither, just desperate to find some plausible excuse for spying on a colleague whilst she showered. He was not diagnosed with either of these conditions at the time of the incident. The cross-examination afterwards is pretty brutal; I feel bad to admit it but it thrills me to watch it. Unsurprisingly, his story just doesn't hold up, as he gets caught in lie after lie after lie. The moment he is most dumbstruck is when our barrister simply asks him 'Why not knock?'

On Day 3, the trial concludes and in the afternoon the jury are sent out to deliberate. They reach no verdict in the little time left that day. All that night Mel and I run the trial over and over in our minds.

On Day 4, jury deliberations resume. For five long hours. Mel and I pace the sun-drenched banks of the River Thames while we wait. It's one of those rare UK summer scorchers that fill everyone with joy and hope, yet here we are agonising and analysing the case over and over, getting more restless with each passing hour. Mel is convinced he will get away with it because they never found an actual picture of her – he deleted it. I worry that it's taking too long: there must be jury members who are on the fence, or perhaps feel uncomfortable wrecking a police officer's career.

With women's safety and a criminal justice system that better protects women in the spotlight, and front and centre of the national conversation, more so than ever in the wake of Sarah's murder, it feels like our whole faith in humanity is hanging in the balance, waiting for justice to be done here.

Finally we're notified that the jury has reached a verdict, so we head back. Even writing this now I feel my adrenalin skyrocket at the thought of those final minutes. As we watch the twelve jury members filter back in to the courtroom, I feel like my heart is pumping so hard that it's rocking me back and forth. They say that when a jury has found a defendant not guilty they will look at them in the dock, but if they have found them guilty they will avoid eye contact. My first glimmer of hope is when I notice that they are not looking in his direction. My second is when they call for the jury spokesperson and a woman stands up. At that moment I felt a slight wave of reassurance.

'Have you reached a verdict upon which you are all agreed? Please answer "yes" or "no".'

'Yes.'

'What is your verdict?'

'Guilty.'

The utter relief of that one word is difficult to describe. It's momentous. We are euphoric. It is such a good feeling to know that the system has worked and he has been brought to justice. He will be on the sex offenders' register for the next five years and receives a twenty-week suspended prison sentence. He'll also undoubtedly be struck off as a police officer pending his misconduct hearing in a few months, but for now he remains suspended on full pay despite being found guilty by the highest criminal court in the land. The delay seems ridiculous but it's not today's concern.

*

Rashid Khan's hearing happened this summer too, more than two years after he first broke into Sana's home late at night. I attended and was glad I did, as the trial went off the tracks when Sana stood up to give evidence but couldn't and wouldn't do it. There were hasty talks about throwing the whole trial out but I begged for her to be treated as a hostile witness (a hostile witness refuses to give evidence in court or gives evidence that differs from their statement), and thankfully the judge agreed. She was then cross-examined by the prosecution on the statement she previously made. It's far from ideal, as it's messy and more traumatic for her, but it results in Rashid being found guilty of burglary and assault. Sana contacted me afterwards. 'I wish I had the chance to go back to court and do it all over again,' she texts. 'I became very nervous when I saw Rashid, it's like he has some power to control what I am saying.' When I tell her I am no longer working for the Met she replies, 'You made women like us feel safe and strong and gave us courage to speak out, it's sad to see you leave.'

Endnote

This wasn't the book I envisaged writing when I pitched the idea. I was early in my journey and my story, the one you've just read, was yet to play out. The most unexpected twist for me was leaving the Met. The book I intended to write was one that bridged the gap between people's fascination with true crime and their lack of insight about what it actually is to be a detective. The one I've written turns out to be far more significant.

I've touched on some huge problems that are harming people, yet can't simply be solved overnight. Awareness of the extent of an issue is a good start, though. There's a saying I love: 'sunlight is the best disinfectant'. I think it's important to illuminate these all-too-often invisible issues by speaking out and sharing individual experiences. Transparency can only be bracingly positive. If no one hears the reality and challenges within their public services and justice system from those who live it, what possible chance is there of things being improved?

When I talk to people about some of the issues I encountered and feel passionately about, I often come up against 'Go on then, what would you do to sort it out?' It's asked as if the problems are so big there is nowhere to start.

For what it's worth, this is what I would do.

1. The Most Urgent: Unlawful CPS charging code which denies women access to justice

Urgent **specific** review of the charging code set out by the Crown Prosecution Service and how rape and domestic abuse are brought to justice in the courts.

Previous reviews come at the issue the wrong way: trying to make the crimes against women fit the existing code and justice system which is clearly — see the stats below — not built for such things. The review needs to start with the crimes against women and adapt the infrastructure of the criminal justice system to effectively work for them.

The current system is not fit for purpose. The way the code is being applied to rape and domestic abuse, crimes predominantly against women, is unlawful and unconstitutional as it blocks these women's access to justice, amounting to systemic misogyny. Additionally, the CPS code frustrates the mission and operational priorities of the Met — to keep London safe for everyone, to focus on what matters most to Londoners (violent crime) and to achieve the best outcomes in the pursuit of justice and in support of victims.

The fact that rape has the lowest charging rate of all crimes is directly correlated to this defect in the criminal justice system. Just 1.3 per cent of 67,125 rape offences recorded in 2021 led to a prosecution. This is no small oversight.

2. Bullies and Bad Apples: Proactive zero tolerance

From my experience officers on the frontline know who the bad apples are but don't speak out. If the Met were to adopt a proactive zero-tolerance process, using a simple anonymous reporting system, they would empower officers to make reports and be able to see the extent of the issue. Instead of turning a blind eye, this proactive approach, putting proper procedures in place, would allow the Met to find the bad apples that tarnish the reputation of the entire organisation, and weed them out. In doing so they would be protecting others from harm.

We ought to learn from #MeToo and #BlackLivesMatter, game-changing movements that unleashed the power of many voices. They empowered people on the receiving end of abuse to give their testimonies, knowing they were not alone. The power of all these accounts, which individually may have been suppressed and ignored when they happened, now reveal an undeniable bigger picture and make the invisible visible. Insidious behaviour suffered for years on end can now be properly exposed.

When Wayne Couzens, a serving Met police officer, murdered Sarah Everard, I kept wondering how no one spotted or reported any warning signs or inappropriate behaviour (he was reportedly nicknamed 'The Rapist', as he made female colleagues feel uncomfortable). Although this is a horrific, unimaginable example, there must be hundreds, thousands of wrong 'uns and bad apples going unchecked and abusing positions of power.

An anonymous reporting system could be used to mark anything that someone considers to be uncomfortable and inappropriate. These warning signs need to be reported and taken seriously.

Take workplace bullying as an example.

There are bullies in workplaces everywhere. I've been on the receiving end from two sergeants while I was a serving police officer in the Met and strangely, while I knew I was being singled out and treated badly, I didn't pinpoint it as bullying for ages until it had really escalated. I think people tend to associate bullying with school and there is more of a stigma around being bullied in the adult world. Workplace bullying is yet another example of unacceptable behaviour that goes unchallenged because – much like sexual assaults in Hollywood, abuse of boys in football, classmate rapes in schools, everyday racism... I could go on – it's one individual's word against the other and the power dynamic usually doesn't favour the complainant, or at least, the perpetrator perceives they are in the position of power.

Workplace bullying

There is no simple definition of bullying because it can take many different forms. However, UNISON has defined workplace bullying as persistent offensive, intimidating, humiliating behaviour, which attempts to undermine an individual or group of employees.

Recognising bullying

Bullying can occur in a number of different ways. Some are obvious and easy to identify. Others are subtle and difficult to explain. Examples of bullying behaviour include:

- Ignoring views and opinions
- Withholding information which can affect a worker's performance
- Setting unreasonable or impossible deadlines
- Setting unmanageable workloads
- Humiliating staff in front of others
- Spreading malicious rumours
- Intentionally blocking promotion or training opportunities
- Ridiculing or demeaning someone by picking on them or setting them up to fail
- Overbearing supervision or other misuse of power or position
- Deliberately undermining a competent worker with constant criticism

Bullying is typical of any abuse in that it's a repeated, targeted pattern of behaviour, so a bully won't strike once in a lifetime and never again. A bully left unchecked will bully over and over again, making a huge number of people's lives a misery over the course of their career.

But, as all these powerful movements have shown, it doesn't need to be one individual's word against another. With a simple independent platform for people to give brief anonymous details using a threshold mechanism (multiple independent reports about the same individual), organisations would be able to identify all the bullies in a very short time.

The form must be as simple and quick to fill out as requesting an Uber (two minutes at the most to fill in enough to submit it) and should allow people to provide as much detail as they feel comfortable with at that time. There is no benefit in re-traumatising people, especially if their testimony might not be properly investigated or actioned until there are multiple reports about the individual in question.

Of course, receiving multiple reports that someone is a bully doesn't immediately prove they are or solve the problem. A proper investigation, resolution and rehabilitation must come next and there needs to be clearer policy around this. All organisations say that bullying is not tolerated but few have a clear policy on what happens to bullies, as it's previously been near-impossible to prove and most people never speak up about it. A hope would also be that in the future this reporting platform would serve as a deterrent, making people think twice about their behaviour, now knowing they can't get away with poor treatment of fellow employees.

3. Closing an Expensive Loophole

This arose in the light of Mel's case, where we learnt that despite being convicted, the officer who committed a serious crime against her would keep every penny of over £100,000 of tax payers' money he had received while suspended on full pay for two and a half years. It's almost a cash incentive to plead not guilty, prolonging the agonising wait for the victim.

Inspired by Gina Miller changing the law around upskirting in a public place, also part of the Voyeurism Act, a group of us have decided to campaign and gather support for an amendment to the existing Proceeds of Crime Act (a piece of legislation which allows seizure of money and assets obtained through crime on conviction) to include public-service workers who are suspended on full pay pending investigation of a crime but later found guilty and convicted. All of the money paid will be seized and re-invested into the organisation.

It isn't right that millions of pounds of public money are kept by criminals while our public services are underfunded. Change is needed.

Training to Become a Detective:
The Syllabus

As the Direct Entry Detective Scheme is brand new we followed the regular police constable foundation course (preparing people to become a PC) with some additional investigative bits tacked on to form our twenty-week training syllabus. We were examined and assessed throughout.

There was a fair bit to get through:

Victim care
Code of ethics
Professionalism
Communication, radios
Pocket-book rules – how to record and write in police style (quite counterintuitive – line through blank space, initials next to crossings out)
Dynamic risk assessment
Diversity, racism, discrimination
Officer safety training (OST)

- OST 1 – powers
- OST 2 – stop and search
- OST 3 – arrest, handcuffs
- OST 4 – CS spray

PACE – police power, custody detention procedures
Theft, robbery, burglary, fraud, handling stolen goods

Assault – all elements including battery, common assault, ABH, GBH

Criminal damage

Sexual offences

Harassment and stalking

Malicious communications

Hate crime

Crime prevention

Radio awareness and procedure – struggle

Suspect identification

Computers and you

Critical incidents

Uniform fitting for Met stab vest and PPE – we do not wear police uniform

Crime scenes, cordons and forensics – Locard's theory and latent fingerprints

Investigation at scenes of crime – building blocks of investigation

Interviewing witnesses and suspects

5-part statement

Safeguarding course – child protection

Mental health – sectioning, mental capacity

Emergency lifesaving course, two days: a whistle-stop tour through at breakneck (sorry) speed – CPR, burns, unconscious, shock, wounds, tourniquet (new word 'necrosis' = tissue dying), motorbike crash victims, choking, seizures, major incident scene management, acid burns

Suicide prevention – a million people a year worldwide kill themselves

Offensive weapons, knives

Drugs, legal highs

Drink driving, taking a conveyance, vehicle interference

Firearms

Powers of search, warrants

Missing persons, aka Mispers

Domestic abuse

Packaging

Investigation scenarios and assessments

Then there are fifty online classes to be done in our own time on further policing procedure and crime areas, such as Modern slavery, Firearms and active shooters, Rape: myth and reality, Kidnap, The dark web, Cyber crime, Terrorism response and many more.

Also, we need to study Blackstone's and learn criminal law inside out and back to front, in more or less its entirety, for the NIE (National Investigators' Exam).

Police Jargon Glossary

Agile	working from home
ANPR	Automatic Number Plate Recognition
Best job in the world	propaganda
Big red button	when someone senior 'hits the big red button' everyone in that borough, or worst case, the entire Met must stay on at work
Big red key	modern battering ram used to gain entry to a property when necessary
Bin – custody	'anyone in the bin?'
Blackout days	there are a few days a year when officers in the Met can't book holiday: Notting Hill Carnival and New Year's Eve/Day
'Blues and twos'	lights and sirens
Body	'I've got a body' – not stating a basic fact but rather 'I'm dealing with a prisoner'
BWV	Body Worn Video – the cameras officers wear to document whatever they attend, on response, planned arrests, etc.
CAD –	Computer Aided Dispatch

CAIT	Child Abuse Investigation Team (I heard this as CAKE for my first few months)
CARM	Computer Aided Resource Manager, booking in and out at the start and end of each shift
Criminal Justice System	The overarching framework of public services which govern custody, court proceedings, conviction, sentencing, probation and resettlement, etc. – how someone is brought to justice
Claret	blood; 'claret everywhere' – bloodbath
Class captain	goodie two shoes and official teacher's pet
Comfort suite	room used to talk to people that's less clinical, more friendly, meant to make them feel more at ease, with a gross sofa and a couple of old toys and picture books
CPS	Crown Prosecution Service – the CPS bring cases against people and decide to charge or not following a police investigation. A separate entity to the police within the CJS
Cradle to grave	one officer keeps a case from the start to the very end
CRIS	Crime Report Information System
Critical incident	the effectiveness of the police response is likely to have a significant impact on the long-term confidence of a victim, family, community, or

even nation. These have the potential to escalate. It's not about the severity of the incident, more about the effectiveness of police. Anyone can declare something as critical

Caution Plus 3	formal interview which takes place at a police station (same as regular interview but without arrest)
Do a door	go to someone's house, bang on door to try to arrest them
Done our legs	stopped us in our tracks – 'CPS have done our legs' – no charge
DP	Detained Person
Full barrier clothing	what you wear to enter a crime scene – booties, throw-away hooded onesie, gloves
ELS	Emergency Life Saving
Emergency	event that threatens serious damage to human welfare
Exhibit	item or object used as evidence of a crime
GAP	Guilty Anticipated Plea
Golden hour	time frame to gather the best evidence following a crime
Guv	another variation on, sarge, sir, skipper, informal for boss
Griefy	see weary
Gucci	fancy
Gutty	complex

IDCOPPLAN	necessity criteria to make an arrest.
Investigation	allow for prompt and effective investigation of an offence
Disappearance	prevent prosecution being hindered by suspect making themself scarce
Child	vulnerable person to protect
Obstruction	Obstruction of highway
Physical	Physical injury to self or others
Public	Public decency
Loss	damage to property
Address	not known
Name	not known
Intimidated victim	common in domestic cases
Jigsaw	management of registered sex offenders in the community
Job	Met word for the force the job has over our lives
Job fit	someone who wouldn't ordinarily be attractive but within the realm of the Met will do
Job pissed	fed up of working in the Met
LAS	Local Ambulance Service
Less than 15	lucrative overtime as not had much notice
Lid	slang for an officer that wears uniform

Major incident	event requiring a response from more than one of the emergency services
MG11	form on which a statement is typed
MO	Modus Operandi – the way in which someone commits their crime. People are creatures of habit and tend to follow the same patterns
MPS	Metropolitan Police Service
Moody	dodgy/stolen
NDOB	Night Duty Occurrence Book
NGAP	Non-Guilty Anticipated Plea
Nick	versatile little word – nickable, arrestable; to nick, to arrest; the nick, home police station
Of good character	no criminal record
Old sweats	old-school detectives nearing retirement
'On' team	response team attending 999 calls
On the hurry up	meaning now! – tends to be used over the radio, e.g. 'We need a van on the hurry up' – means we have arrested someone and need to be collected asap, except everyone says it so it means nothing
Osmon warning	delivering one of these is letting someone know their life is in danger
Over the side	cheating, sleeping with someone else

Pink and fluffy	a derogatory term for soft skills in the police such as communication and empathy
Pod	locker
Positive action	doing something, usually interpreted as arrest
PPE	the ordinary police PPE comprises a stab vest, pockets stuffed full of blue latex gloves, clip-on belt with handcuffs, pepper spray canister and extendable baton
Remand	place in custody
Restricted duties	no longer let loose on the public but desk-based, either because being on the frontline might harm you (e.g. if pregnant or recovering from illness) or because you pose a potential risk to the public (e.g. if under investigation or on performance review)
Rocking horse shit	rare, very hard to get hold of
Refs	short for refreshment – break, lunch
Rest days	days off – this is a 24/7 job so there is no right to getting evenings and weekends off any more Self ref – take your break when you want
Sarge	short for sergeant
Shit magnet	an individual who has a collection of bizarre, disgusting, odd tales because what they deal with is never quite straightforward

Skipper	informal for boss
Slag	no-hoper criminal, repeat offender – derogatory yet very commonly used word
Smashed the arse out of the OT	did a LOT of overtime
Stuck on	internally punished, put on the naughty step
Tasty	shit hits the fan
War and peace	writing something really long – 'I'm not asking for War and Peace' (subtext: keep it concise)
Weary	annoying, admin-heavy, dull, endless task which is not going anywhere or doing anybody any good, least of all the executor
'Welcome to the Met'	tough shit, get used to it

Acknowledgements

With Thanks To

All who've championed me and this book it's been a long time coming and you've carried me through.

Fran and Jane for reading and believing in my moonshot proposal, taking it on, through a bidding war and getting me this book deal. Everyone I've worked with and those behind the scenes at Bloomsbury who've been involved in creating the book and putting it out into the world with a bang; particularly Alison, Katie, Francisco and Hayley. A special mention to Victoria, my book doctor and saviour of this project. All your enthusiasm, help and skill was instrumental at a point when I was ready to throw in the towel. Working with you restored my faith and confidence so I can't thank you enough for that.

On to the people in the book; The Orphanarium crew – Rachie, Paddy, Evie, Maddie, Lucy and James. You guys are my beloved London family. Rachie and Paddy you have been so good to me, taking me in like a stray so many times. Living with you and any reunion since is such a joy... 'That's why we ride'. Olie, I'm sorry there is no flaming warrant card on the front cover – it was out of my hands. Essex life with you was fab, you've always been there for me with a dose of brutal honesty and humour. Rob, Doug, Tom and Birdy for brightening my police days. Lexi T and Mel, we were in it together and our friendships are without doubt the best thing to come out of my time in the Met.

All my friends who've been such a big support to me these past years. I'm quite a crap friend. Useless at keeping in touch, remembering birthdays, turning up on time or at all. But despite this, I really hope you know how important you are to me. Especially Char, Dave, Katie, Sazzy, Ro, Bex and Julia – you've been legends to share this experience with and helped me more than you know during the rough bits. Also to the whole Eckersley and Platt family for taking such good care of me that particularly bleak winter.

My family at large; Bigglestones, Wrights, Brownings, McDonalds, Blakemores … all of my aunts, uncles and cousins, I adore you all. I feel extremely lucky to be a part of this enormous, close-knit clan.

My immediate family – Mum, Dad, Tom, Angus, Hannah and Jess – I simply couldn't ask for better people. Growing up with you has allowed me to become the fine specimen you see before you today! You've put up with me beautifully. Mum and Dad you are selflessly there for me every step of the way. You always told me the sky was the limit but you didn't mind what I did or became as long as it made me happy and then gave me everything I needed to set off on my rather random journey. People say I'm brave to have opened up and written this but I'm only able to give things a go and take leaps of faith because I feel so secure in your love and support. I know whatever I try I can't really fall and I think that's the greatest foundation you can give a person. Thank you for being my constants, I love you all eternally.

Finally, to the man whose creative flair gave us Warwick Shandy. Phil, you're the love of my life, my soulmate, best friend and a jester all rolled into one. I've never met a person as wonderful as you before (No, I wasn't expecting that). Not only are you a stunner, a worldie, a sorrrrrrrrrrrrrrrrrrrrrrrt but extremely bright, funny as they come, kind, caring and honourable to your core. In other words, you're a fucking catch. Life with you is heaven and how I want to spend the rest of my days. Whatever happens we're in it together so cheers to you! (uno mas?) I love you so much.

A Note on the Author

Jess McDonald grew up in Cheshire, attended Durham University and had a huge range of jobs before she turned 30. Then the big one. At the age of 31, Jess was one of the very first people to gain a place on the Met Police's controversial Direct Entry Detective scheme and, after just 5 months of training, started work as a Detective Constable tackling serious crime in a busy east London borough.

A Note on the Type

The text of this book is set in Joanna, a transitional serif type-face designed by Eric Gill (1882–1940) in the period 1930–31, and named for one of his daughters. The typeface was originally designed for proprietary use by Gill's printing shop, Hague & Gill. The type was first produced in a small quantity by the Caslon Foundry for hand composition. It was eventually licensed for public release by the Monotype foundry in 1937.